A MATTER OF DISTANCE

Lessons from a Pandemic

By Gail Vetter Levin

MIRADA

PRESS

ISBN 979-8-9899877-0-2

Cover art and design by Danielle Kasum
Page design by katsatori89
Author photo by Michelle Berkowitz

Independently published by Mirada Press

distance

noun

dis· tance ˈdi-stən(t)s

1: the quality or state of being distant

    a: spatial remoteness

    b: personal and emotional separation

    c: difference, disparity

2: separation in time

    the degree or amount of separation between two points,

    lines, surfaces, or objects

verb

distanced; distancing

1: to make or keep an emotional separation from

2: to leave far behind

Merriam-Webster Dictionary

Dedication

For Manhattan born Mirabel Joy and San Diego born Ada Lou. From a distance and up close, they make life infinitely sweeter. And up close is better.

Contents

March 2020

"People say nothing is impossible, but I do nothing every day."

~Winnie the Pooh

Day 1

Mirabel Joy is fifteen months old—a whip-smart, pixie-haired, animated toddler. The world, including her world in Brooklyn, has shut down: the grocery shelves are nearly empty, sirens are a constant, and playing outdoors is forbidden. Her much-loved nanny has been deemed "non-essential" and sent home. The neighborhood where everyone knows her is empty of those sweet, familiar faces. An urban ghost town. Her parents, who kissed her good-bye each morning as they headed for the M train into Manhattan, well…they're just upstairs—one working in the guest room, the sunny side, which sizzles, and the other in the master, looking out at the winter trees. That room stays cold. They take turns working and tending to their whip-smart, pixie-haired, animated toddler, Mirabel.

Her grandfather and I are 2,863 miles away, tucked comfortably into an old Spanish house in San Diego that is always the right temperature but so, so far from Mirabel.

It's March 15th, 2020 and a whole lot of "Who the hell knows" is barreling toward us.

~

Yesterday's *The New York Times* headline: EMERGENCY IS DE-CLARED; HOUSE PASSES AID BILL. The worst-case scenario for this disease, according to the Center for Disease Control: between 200,000 and 1.7 million deaths in the United States. Today's front page: the Pope has declared Holy Week services will not be open to the public, the Masters Golf tournament and the Boston Marathon have been cancelled, Louisiana and Georgia primaries will be delayed. Spain is in a nationwide lockdown. California Governor Gavin Newson has declared all California schools closed. In three days, we are ordered to stay at home.

I was in seventh grade when we were at the brink of nuclear war with Russia. Something big and terrifying was happening. Bomb shelters were built, basements were stocked. My mom, a pragmatist to the end, drew her own red line: "I'm not going to be on the clean-up committee." On brand for my mom but lacking comfort to her twelve-year-old daughter. The Vetters would have no bomb shelter. Clean up would be left to the others. The ominous pall we feel right now is eerily reminiscent of that time, and I fret for all of us—especially Mirabel Joy.

My husband was a television newsman—award winning, as they say. He could read three pages and tell you the only four points that mattered, and then he would share those four points on television, speaking to thousands of people who believed they could trust him. They were right. He's retired now. His keen interest and boundless acumen have waned. You can tell the world how bad it is for only so many years before you want to take a serious break, and retirement has proven to be just that. He's still crazy smart but no longer the "go to" that insured his career and my calm in the past. We'll have to learn together what news matters and what is just noise.

My part, through myriad careers, has been to make the home. Always was and will be even more right now. I will gather the necessities, make the meals, keep us comfortable and clean. And keep the record. Journals, lists, quips—those are my comfort and calling. These times offer plenty of fodder.

Our child, J.T., our best and only, lives on the other side of the country with Kate, his beautiful wife, and that irresistible baby girl. When you type in Mirabel's name, it often autocorrects to "Miracle," and it's not wrong. J.T. and Kate have thriving careers in tech, demanding but satisfying. Their home is warm and welcoming. My son has it all—a family he adores, a job that matters, and a community that goes nearly as fast as he does. New York suits them.

But New York now stands at the heart of what has officially been declared a global pandemic. My kids are in the thick of it but none of us, even those of us nearly 3,000 miles away, will escape the wrath of COVID-19.

Things are quiet in San Diego right now. Occasional cars, sirens. Rare walkers—most of them wearing scrubs. With two hospitals near-by, I wonder about how things look inside them. Calm before the storm or frantic preparation or has the chaos begun? Are workers frightened or energized or exhausted? It feels like a secret.

We saw our sweet neighbors in the driveway yesterday; they wanted us to know that if we needed anything they would be happy to run an errand or fill a request for food. In that moment I realized we have become "those people"—the ones I always tried to help with a casserole or a call. That kindness, gratefully accepted, has a double edge. One side: we have loving neighbors. The other side: we are old.

A friend of ours who is an M.D. with a Master's in Public Health—and twenty years working in preventive medicine at the Center for Disease Control—sent a long note warning us about what's ahead. "It's time to hunker down," the subject line reads; she makes a case for preparing ourselves for a long and uncertain road.

As a professor at the University of California San Diego now, she said she's grateful that school is closing down and students are being sent home but admits that it's a massive task.

You can imagine the havoc this wreaks. UCSD stands to lose $30M on campus housing refunds alone, and my poor students (literally) are going to lose a huge amount because they have fixed apt leases until the end of the school year, not to mention their jobs on campus which are keeping many of them from starving. Argh!

She ends the note: *Bon courage—think we are in for what may be one of the most trying times in our lives. Nancy*

Why does it feel like it's all happening so fast? We'd been hearing about a viral threat for a few weeks without having any sense of our part in it…a story about sick people on cruise ships and a shortage of PPE—whatever that is—and so many random references to China.

Our Neighborhood Watch group was getting together on Monday, as usual. "Dawn will discuss Corvid-19 (sic)," the email announcement read, "the disease caused by the corona virus. We are fortunate to have our own neighborhood infectious disease epidemiologist."

We gathered at Bob and Carol's for Corona Sunrises, a happy concoction of beer, tequila, and orange juice. I shared mine with a neighbor and we laughed about cooties.

Then, in an instant, the tone changed.

With Dawn's handout, our learning curve about NOVEL COVID-19 began. "Novel" (never seen before), "COVID" (Corona Virus category), 19 (first discovered in 2019). Daunting information that Dawn, always light and warm, shared with sober urgency. No soft sell here. She's smart, she's informed, and she's worried.

We should save masks for the medical professionals unless we're older. *(We are older.)* She means it. Get gloves, get Lysol. Get ready—it's coming. No Corona Sunrise was strong enough to lighten the mood.

The next day I did some thoughtful marketing. Meat, chicken, rice, beans, coffee, soup. Sensible basics. Lysol and toilet paper. Toilet paper has become an issue. Somehow everyone has panicked about toilet paper. I started out with two large six-packs stashed under the cart, but by the time I got to check-out, just one remained. The other pack had slipped off, probably retrieved by another grateful shopper. The universe was telling me to settle down and share nicely.

J.T. called from New York to see if we were ready. His words were pressing, his tone frightened. "This is no joke, Mom. You need to have two weeks' worth of food and then I don't want you or Dad to leave the house for anything. Nothing! I need for you to promise." Shrill ambulance sirens blared in his background through the entire call, so he didn't hear my soft, "I promise."

The lead-up after that felt like a slow march. Not immediate but looming cancellations. Many events that shared one conversation.

"Are you worried?"

"How crazy is this?"

"We won't get to do this again for awhile" conversations. We feared for our Barcelona trip in May, stayed positive that Alaska in July would still happen. We felt sure our outdoor summer symphony tickets were secure, but maybe not next month's Old Globe Theatre (an inside venue). We were confident that our nearby hospitals would be ample for the urban population, but we were concerned for folks in remote areas.

Quiet speculation and then sinister acceleration. Tom Hanks and Rita Wilson have it! Disneyland is shuttered! March Madness Basketball has been cancelled!

This shit just got real.

Day 2: March 16, 2020

I needed to hear my son's voice so I sent a text asking for a phone call when he could. He called back quickly and started with, "Please tell me you don't have bad news. Are you ok? Is Dad?"

It's how we all feel now. The shoe waiting to drop. The *"They're heeere…"* moment. Waves of dread followed, a bit later, as I remember that life isn't normal. I'm feeling guilty for not getting anything done during this amazing luxury of time and then remember, "Oh yeah. There's a global pandemic," kind of like, "Oh yeah. I still need to go to the market," or "Oh yeah. I meant to call her."

My first pandemic-era tears came this evening when I panicked worrying about my sort-of-brother. Mark, a bestie-like-family since our teenage years, is on a short list of friends who are still working. I realized how vulnerable he is at the Farmer's Market in Los Angeles—a place he manages brilliantly by sharing warm relationships with vendors and customers alike. I called him; he was working from home. I breathed. I told him I didn't think I could bear it if he got sick and he soothed me in the way that he can—as a brother, a loving adult—and said he'd be fine. I have to believe him because, I just do. I'd forgotten how much I love his voice.

Focus on the practical, I thought as I inventoried the medicine cabinet. I've laid in zinc tablets and NyQuil—useful for the light cases, so they say, and I'll make room for that. Just that. I read that a humidifier might be helpful so Amazon is on it. I've been craving fresh fruit. Costco's delivery, Instacart, will arrive in six days between 1:00 and 2:00. I feel great pride at getting on their schedule. What a curious reaction.

Day 3: March 17, 2020

I took a walk with Susan near the pier. Downtown streets were abandoned of cars and the bay, usually bright and calm, looked restless and gray. I thought of the 1959 movie *On the Beach* about the end of the world. Set in Australia, the characters find the best way to manage their final days before the fallout of a nuclear exchange annihilates them. I saw it when that was the great fear—the world ending with a bang. This feels like a whisper.

Associated Press announced that Kaiser Permanente has begun testing experimental vaccines with forty-five volunteers taking two shots each month. "We're all a team now," their CEO said. We've already lapsed to cliches. "We're all in this together" could drive us mad before this is over.

Yesterday, the U.S. stock market fell to its lowest point since 1987. Hospitals have begun canceling all elective procedures and Amazon is experiencing unprecedented volume.

In the midst of all this dire direction, one news story is a feel-good. The animal shelters in San Diego have been emptied. No pups, no cats, not a pit-bull or a guinea pig. Those owners that hadn't been brave enough before found their courage with the lock-down.

That would include us!

Yup, we have a sweet new puppy who is oblivious to all the pain around her. This quiet world is the only one she has ever known.

I should back up…

A few days before the world locked down, we realized that all our trips had been cancelled, all our activities postponed, and all our "we'd like a dog but can't get one because…" excuses were suspended. If this quarantine was indefinite, the time might be right and the company might be nice. We should get a dog. We headed to the animal shelter where we found lots of folks who had the same idea. And we found Poppy. Three months old. Lab/Beagle (probably) mix. Sweet, shy, and awfully pretty. She's a Lab. What could go wrong?

As others assembled their food, jigsaw puzzles, books, Netflix lists and toilet paper, we added dog food to our list and settled in with our pup. Mirabel will love her. Hope Poppy is still a pup when they finally meet.

Day 4: March 18, 2020

For all my nervous efforts last week, my grocery shopping was pretty haphazard. No great edible combinations and I'm wishing for a do-over. I'd gathered comfort food like chips and ice cream, and Red Vines and oatmeal. Some poultry and hamburger but I gave no real thought or imagination to the culinary efforts ahead.

Today, I went to the market, curiosity shrouded in an excuse of necessity. I wanted soup. Soup needs onions. Vons has onions. I calculated every step in a way I never have before. Take my own bags, of course. Check for too many cars, skip the cart, avoid aisles that have other people, use a glove for the doors—all firsts. So many never-befores. Aisles with no goods or few goods or goods for which even the desperate have no need—loofas, cranberry salad, plastic cups. No pasta. No ice cream. (Seriously?) Lots of sandwich bags and vinegar.

The cashier, Roberta, checked me out with "just fine" to my question about how she's doing. "Or I was until yesterday when I had the day off and got caught up on the news." And then Roberta had to come back to sell me onions and probably take abuse no one deserves with fears few have known. I put a twenty-dollar bill on the counter and said, "Nobody deserves a tip more…" and before I could finish the sentence, she said, "Oh no! I'd lose my job!" She startled me. But of course. But unfair. And then she said, "Your offer is a big gift. That means so much to me." The exchange took moments but it broke my heart.

A cartoon is making the rounds: "In a few more weeks, we will all know what our friend's natural hair color is." Truth and humor. Funny until I remember that includes me. I wonder how I'll look in white.

Day 5: March 19, 2020

I walked to our neighborhood bakery, Bread & Cie, today. I didn't expect them to be open but they were and it made me so happy. Two petit French loaves. For the soup. Taking tiny little chances and hoping they are tiny enough.

China has expelled U.S. journalists, a poll taken by NPR indicates that 60% of the population does not trust the president in matters of the virus and two members of Congress have COVID.

Day 6: March 20, 2020

A poem has gone viral on the internet.
And people stayed home and read books and listened
and rested and exercised and made art and played
and learned new ways of being
and stopped and listened deeper

someone meditated someone prayed
someone danced someone met their shadow
and people began to think differently
and people healed
and in the absence of people who lived in ignorant ways,
dangerous, meaningless and heartless,
even the earth began to heal
and when the danger ended and people found each other
grieved for the dead people
and they made new choices and dreamed of new visions
and created new ways of life and healed the earth completely
just as they were healed themselves.

~Kitty O'Meara

What if COVID-19 marked a turning point in kindness and conservation and connection?

There's a Hebrew prayer that asks for a blessing of peace and understanding. It translates roughly to "May it be so" or even "Amen."
Kein Y'hi Ratzon.

Day 7: March 21, 2020

It's a gorgeous day in San Diego. My friend Marilyn and I took a walk—our new normal walk. No shared burrito or jostling on the sidewalk or trading phones to share pictures. She managed the street side, damn near in the middle of the road, until I demanded a compromise of walking single file with six feet between us. Balboa Park was teaming with runners and bicycle riders and so many dogs happy to be out. People are not in clusters and some masks are in evidence but it would be easy to mistake the day for any other until you look closely. We found a shady bench and sat apart from each other as we discussed everything from family worries to book editing.

Her friendship, the sunshine, the beauty of the day make me so grateful. Just simple gratitude. Overheard as we walked by a pair of men in lively conversation, "I'm gay. I've been social distancing since I was four!" Little gifts.

Day 8: March 22, 2020

We have lived in this new world for a week and at moments, it all feels fine. And nearly over. And accomplished.

It's not.

Day eight with our puppy and she's a great source of joy. Marty might argue with that but his actions scream the fact, especially when they are curled up for a nap. They both love a nap. Poppy also loves her crate, her corner of the patio, and her snuggles on the sofa. She doesn't love her walk away from the house. As soon as we head for home, she's in the Iditarod ready, again, to shelter in place!

Big day at our house. A dog walk and my Costco order. At the appointed time, in real time, I shopped with Jose. He was at Costco. I was home. Our love language was by text.

We were such a team. Apparently, only one rotisserie chicken is allowed per customer (I had asked for two) and he had to swap our flank steak for a tri-tip. I assured him it was no problem. Was it too late to ask him to add asparagus? He was delighted to. These silly exchanges made me ridiculously happy and sharply aware of how lucky I am. Apples, blueberries, water, copier paper, coffee. Jose is on it all and all in Costco sizes. I have enough mayonnaise for three summers of potato salad and enough tuna to sink a boat.

We'll share some of this with Arlene so I'm especially pleased that they had some of the things she loves. My friend is still a full time Rabbi overseeing a large congregation. She is almost helpless in some of the practical things that have never been hard for me, like planning ahead and taking care of herself, but she is gifted beyond measure in ways that matter most, like taking care of others. This morning she led a virtual funeral for a family who lost a child. Beyond my comprehension. I think she gets the rotisserie chicken.

Emails, texts, and FaceTime have taken on new life. The technology that ended so much personal communication has now become the lifeline and we're all trying to sort out our time and resources, alone and with others. My friend Alicia captured it like this:

I'm wishing you laughter and accomplishment of your choice during our forced internment. May our isolation work to save lives so people can return quickly to their jobs and the ability to feed and house their families. And may laughter prevail inside the close quarters that we are keeping these days with loved ones. May we still love them when this is over.

I'm not really one to pray but if I were, I'd be focused on Italy right now. Over five thousand have died there. And prayers for nursing homes. They are in the strictest lockdowns with ambulances omnipresent. And I'd pray for the doctors, nurses, janitors.

And the cashiers.

Day 9: March 23, 2020

Mirabel threw us kisses on FaceTime.
COVID cases just surpassed 300,000 globally.
I haven't washed my hair for four days.

Day 11: March 25, 2020

My work pattern has been a constant in my life: Procrastination, Guilt, Productivity. Repeat. I was raised to be busy. Any alternative was unacceptable—even shameful. Show your work and get on to the next task. Be accountable and at the end of the day, measure your worth by how far you've made it down the list. I don't have any memory of my parents relaxing. My dad read, voraciously, but even that was a measure of pages covered or depth of understanding gained. Mom cooked to relax but always to produce something delicious like coconut cake or homemade noodles or a pie—especially a pie.

There was never, ever an option of doing nothing. Small voices were always whispering, "What's next?" In this strange pause we're in, it's become easier to procrastinate, ignore the guilt. Harder to be productive. I'm in constant conflict about it.

I washed my hair. Something.

Day 12: March 26, 2020

FaceTime. Thank goodness. The highpoint of any day: watching our granddaughter as she commands their small quarters in Brooklyn. She held up a "phone" to talk to us today. It was a tube of Desitin and we chatted on.

Frightening news from the New York region: with over half of the country's illnesses it's being called the epicenter of the virus and the panic is just beginning. There will not be enough caregivers or places to give care to all those who need help. The hardest choices will follow. Who can live and who can die. The starkness is chilling. Temporary morgues are stationed nearby—all just a few doors away from where my little Mirabel eats her oatmeal and practices her fish face.

I have watched the president's briefing every day. I don't know if I am more heartbroken or angry at the inept, self-absorbed man who is leading us through this crisis. When history writes this story, chapters will be dedicated to his ignorance, deceit, and psychosis. This virus and this president created the perfect storm and we could not have seen this level of destruction without them arriving in concert.

My friend Tom, never a raging optimist, recently expressed deeper concern than usual. As a scientist with initials after his name, he gets his say. When I pressed him, he finally said, "We'll get through it, but it's gonna leave a mark."

I'm left to wonder how disfiguring that mark will be.

Day 15: March 29, 2020

Yesterday, Marty and I took the dog for a ride. She had never seen the ocean and didn't much care either way—but I did. I needed a fix and it was more magnificent than ever. Not a soul near the water. Yellow tape blocking the entrance. Even the ocean is closed.

Folks were walking and riding and driving—all a respectful distance from others. A young couple sat on the side of their truck looking out to the view and eating salads. I want to imagine that they are a young couple, recently married, who can't believe their luck at being quarantined just now. I'd like to think they crawled out of bed just long enough to eat a bite and breathe the ocean air before getting naked and going back undercover. It would be nice if this was a glorious time for someone.

I had a major meltdown a few nights ago when J.T. called. We Face-Time'd with wide-eyed Mirabel but, just this once, her animated image was overshadowed by my anguished and exhausted son. They had just found out they have bedbugs—a horrid little beast that hasn't killed anyone but has made a lot of lives miserable. The creatures are mostly confined to the guest room but, for my son, it was the last straw. He and his wife are struggling to support their companies (anyone who isn't is the rare exception), they are home 24/7 with a fifteen-month-old who, while precious, needs constant attendance. They are living in the hotspot for this contagion and now they have a challenge that, if all the others were not present, would still be a monumental pain in the ass.

Every mother knows that she can handle pretty much anything if her kids are okay. Mine were not. And there was nothing I could do to help.

If only I were there.

If only they were here.

I haven't let myself think much about what a dangerous place New York is right now, but in the moments after the phone call, I gave in to it and felt genuine panic. I sent a note asking them to please consider a flight to San Diego. I made the case with links to articles about the empty planes and how clean they are, charts on how to travel taking the fewest risks, advice about masking a toddler. I told him how we'd manage it at the house and that we would all be safe—or safer—and we would make it work.

"Your dad and I are healthy and strong," I wrote, "and we've been self-quarantined for two weeks. Risk to us is minimal and manageable. Mirabel is not at risk, according to all statistics. We have red carpet access to medical care if anyone needs it. You could both work twelve hours a day from here."

I kept going. "I'm not just an emotional grandma. I just think it's a viable option you should at least consider with Kate. We just want you safe."

I pushed "send" and then hoped—not quite certain what I was hoping for.

Fact is, there were many reasons for them to say no, which they did. The one that matters to them is that they might expose us, especially Marty who is in the higher-risk category, so it was a hard "no." Hard for me, especially, since I would take any risk. Any. If I knew it would keep them safe.

Day 17: March 31, 2020

This isn't fun anymore.

To be clear, it was never fun but it was interesting and novel and fascinating in a macabre sort of way. Today it felt dark and real and, yes, scary. The President has stopped saying that this is manageable. He's making others say the hard stuff, but at least he's not arguing. Dr. Deborah Birx, the physician brought in as White House Coronavirus Response Coordinator, minced no words: "If we get this right… if we do everything perfectly, we can keep the deaths to somewhere between 100,000 and 240,000 people."

This week, New York's death toll exceeded 1,000. Italy surpassed 20,000.

My calendar mocked me with a reminder that I have a 7:10am flight to JFK Airport in the morning. Except I don't. I ate a scoop of ice cream—as I have most nights.

Screw it.

April 2020

"Be safe, be smart, be kind."

~Dr. Tedros Adhanom Ghebreyesus, World Health
Organization Director General

Day 21: April 4, 2020

So many head-spinning changes while so much stays still. This window may bring back poetry and classical music as we all pay more attention to life's exquisite details. The simple sounds and sights we usually miss—a chattering bird or sunning gecko, the cadence in a mother's cooing to her child as they pass in the stroller or the faint wind chime a few houses away. It has been a sensory deficit and overload all at once. You hear phrases like "deafening silence" and "calm chaos" and "frightening stillness." Poets must ache for moments like this.

J.T. and Kate still slog through mud in New York. Their stressful days and nights are set against a backdrop of stillness and a symphony of sirens. Their nerves must feel like chewed pieces of rope. Careers in technology make their remote mandate easier but nothing else about their lives is. Start-ups all over the world are stretched thin with this learning curve. J.T. and Kate are in leadership positions which means juggling balls of fire with their jobs and family. When my son calls and I can get Mirabel's full attention, I see him steal the few moments, seconds really, to rest—although it's not fair to call it that. No wind-down option exists for any of them right now. Little Mirabel, because it's her job to demand full attention. J.T. and Kate because the world is in crisis.

An artist friend of mine brought out all of her paintings today and, in chalk on the sidewalk, announced an art show: an unusual and sweet distraction.

The San Diego Union Tribune's front page today featured four articles: swimming and surfing in the ocean is prohibited; there have been one thousand local cases of Corona virus with seventeen deaths; follow these illustrations and instructions to sew a face mask; and an executive order signed by New York's governor to seize unused ventilators.

There is no sports section.

Day 22: April 5, 2020

Occasionally, I try to imagine how the world will be in one year. We are living in a turning point. But what direction? According to Johns Hopkins University, the number of coronavirus cases worldwide just exceeded 1.1 million.

I'm out of ice cream!

Day 23: April 6, 2020

J.T. sent a picture of Mirabel wandering their little kitchen corridor wearing the rabbit ears headband I sent to her. It lights up. So does she.

Day 25: April 8, 2020

I went to the market yesterday. Old folks' hour at 7 am. I was geared up with a mask, gloves, and glasses—standard dress code now for most of us. But not all of us. Why do some choose to defy what seems to be common wisdom now? Do they feel invincible? No one that qualifies for that time slot at Von's is invincible. Are they non-believers who think it is blown out of proportion? That makes them idiots, to my mind, and I presume they've pickled their brains on Fox news.

Maybe it's not that complicated and they just felt like making a dash. Taking a chance. We all are, almost all the time. Open the front gate, let the possibilities in. Best and worst analogy I've heard: the virus is like glitter. You can have one little sparkle on your face, and it can stick for days. If someone has glitter on their face, it drives me nuts! *Gawd.* I hate fucking glitter. Guess that's the point.

Yet I risked the virus, the glitter, for chicken stock and toilet paper and butter and sweet potatoes.

And ice cream.

Day 26: April 9, 2020

We shared a lovely seder table with seven other families. The candlesticks were from Marty's family and rich with history: buried in Lithuania before WWII and retrieved years after. They are precious to us. The seder plate had all the elements from horseradish to matzah. Wine for me and grape juice for Marty.

All the other families seemed to have the same —the Zoom boxes were small so it's hard to know for certain.

The central question of the Seder asks what it means to be free. It's a worthy question any year and especially this one. Maya Angelou said, "The truth is, no one of us can be free until everybody is free." The question this year: freedom from what?

"Next year in Jerusalem," a phrase often sung at the end of the Passover Seder, to which I will add: "...or at least together."

Day 27: April 10, 2020

When J.T. was in college, he and his bestie, Brian, started a silk-screening business—*Duds by Dudes*. I think their success surprised them both, but after college, it was Brian who stayed the course and turned that little lemonade stand into a significant business.

A few weeks ago, I had the sad task of helping Brian draft a lay-off notice to the employees he loves. Since screening a T-shirt doesn't qualify as an essential service, he needed to tell thirty employees that they didn't have a job. We worked hard on the letter, hoping it could comfort even as it devastated. But then this resourceful young man got an idea. If he could secure enough masks, which are essential, and convince enough customers to imprint them, he might keep DUDS alive and his people employed. He just sent me a note asking me to spread the word. He has 10,000 masks now and could lock-in 200,000 by the end of the week. Printing cost, of course, depends on the quantity.

When most of us are whining about finding toilet paper, my young friend has found thousands of masks and saved dozens of jobs. Gotta love American ingenuity.

Day 29: April 12, 2020

Easter Sunday brought to you by Zoom—the new community gathering place. I'm curious to see if it remains a noun or becomes a verb or returns to an adjective. On any given meeting, three Zoom boxes are nicely manageable. Four are okay but you'll struggle a bit. On my first Zoom today, we had seven boxes. Family members in each one but Aunt Donna had two boxes—one for her elbow. One cousin had a mike that didn't work, one had the mute that couldn't be clicked and one had the image that never focused. And Aunt Donna's elbow. One cousin, recently widowed, is heart broken and her little box was bathed in gray.

My large family has shared many Easters over the years. Easter egg hunts and new frocks with crinolines and Easter bonnets. Family pictures and big ham dinners. Simpler times. Today we have some real differences that we feel about this time, this virus, its demands and the political chaos. I love my family but we are a fragmented lot and our struggle with technology felt like a metaphor for our challenging communication today.

My second Zoom was with the high school gang. I adore these people and have for a long time. The catch-ups are full of inside jokes and belly laughs. We can't go deep, though. As much as some of us crave a meaningful political conversation, the conservative bent of one keeps that from happening. We're all trying to respect "the rule" of no politics but life is so damn political right now and the impacts so profound. How do we not talk about the president and the policies and the insanity we're all watching? But we try.

Zoom #3 was with New York. Our kids are hanging tough so we must, too. Precious Mirabel can put on her own hat. Really! A big brown knit cap that swallows her up until she gets her big brown eyes out from under it. Putting on your own hat is a pretty big deal when you think about it. She's sixteen months! Truly remarkable. And she can say their dog's name, Maggie. How far can she be from "Grammy?" How long before she can say it to me? For all the joy of that Zoom, I'm left with an ache that is only slightly less than my worry.

Day 31: April 14, 2020

According to the Washington Post, churches all over the country defied COVID isolation orders and held in-person services on Easter morning. So, we'll see. Meantime, Disney World just laid off 43,000 employees and New York has updated their COVID fatalities to over 10,000.

None of that news kept us from a riotous evening with neighbors.

Beth and her wife, Sara, along with Mark, Marty and I (we make up the three houses in our row dating back to 1922, '25 and '26) held a six-feet-apart-bring-your-own-food-beverages-utensils-salt-and-pepper-matzah-and-parsley Seder on the patio. The laughter, levity, unleavened bread, candles and stories about growing up Jewish (all but Beth and me) made for a most wonderful and most welcome night. It felt so good to laugh that much again.

Finally, amazing news for our kids. Mirabel's beloved nanny has asked to return to work. They've been paying her—it was the right thing to do and "non-essential" wasn't her idea —but she called and said she missed them all so much and could she be in a pod with them? Pods have caught on quickly as people decide who to isolate with, even from separate households. Kate's brother, also in the pod, will drive her back and forth (he's a laid off restaurant worker) so J.T. and Kate can focus on work. Happy, happy day!

Day 32: April 15, 2020

More neighbors. This time Tess, six and Kendrick, nine. I offered to watch them for a few hours to give their mom and dad a short break. It's been about six weeks of remote learning, aka school, and I don't think you could find a parent who isn't exhausted and over it. The three of us found ways to pass the time but, without being able to be inside or get too close to them, it was a challenge. Mother May I, Simon Says and a few art projects offered a nice change but I'm pretty sure they were ready to go home when it was time. The note from their mom said, "I had a chance to do yoga and finish my book. Simply heaven."

Remote learning is a hot topic as hundreds of thousands of kids spend their day staring at a screen. Articles stress that parents have to establish a routine, try to find ways to make it fun and trust the teachers. All of this assumes that a kid has a computer, that a kid has a printer and that—biggest of all—a kid has caring parents that are managing all of this for them.

If school resumed tomorrow, there would still be so much that's been lost for these children and the hard fact is that it's not going to resume any time soon.

Day 35: April 18, 2020

We're doing our own remote learning with Poppy and a dog trainer. Marty and I meet with her—on Zoom—as she walks us through the training moves with our little pup. It's about basic commands so I'm not sure that the remote part is a big hindrance but this sweet little pup is showing herself to be far more energetic and assertive than we had counted on. So we pace the patio with little treats in our pocket—a firm tug when she's off course and a piece of hot dog when she gets it right, all the while wondering, "What have we done?"

Day 36: April 19, 2020

I cleaned out my car today. It was a time capsule. Weeks old dry-cleaning I didn't drop off and will need who knows when. Flip-flops for an intended (but cancelled) pedicure. Borrowed gloves and cap for our Alaska trip and a book about Barcelona for the adventure in Spain. Sigh. Oh, and a mini diet Coke. I was being disciplined then. That was then. I order the thirty can twelve-ounces now. So there.

Time will come later to resuscitate my self-discipline. Probably about the same time that I get in the car and go somewhere besides the grocery store.

Day 38: April 21, 2020

Saturday was a walk with Marilyn, one of my favorite things; a backyard visit with Arlene which was a sweet surprise; and a six-foot apart dinner with a young couple which felt a little like having our kids over. No hugs, no close contact, but by bedtime I wondered if I had truly tempted the fates. There is such a strange fear that is the foundation of all we do right now. Even collecting the mail makes my heart race a little. Wash your hands. Hope for the best. Imagine how those who have to have contact and so, have much more to fear, are coping.

I'm reading through my dad's letters home during WWII. He was a kid in a situation I can't fathom. Being shot at, shooting at others. The letters are yellowed and brittle but the writing is brilliant, tender and funny. One from July 1944 was written the day that Saipan surrendered to the Americans. My dad had been in active combat. He closes with assurances to his "Mom and Pop."

"You can quit worrying now. The campaign is over and unless I fall down and break my neck, I'm safe as can be. Goodnight. Love to all, Tom."

I guess that coping is almost always about time and place.

Day 42: April 25, 2020

42. Jeez! When I wrote Day 1, we thought it was a two-week lockdown. It's been six. Six weeks of not doing much which means our version of a lockdown has been pretty manageable because there hasn't been much we needed to do.

I'm surprised to find comfort in the sameness. Even through these weeks, I have favorite days and times of day and moments in those times. I like weekdays more than weekends. I like 2:00 more than noon. I like bedtime but don't mind morning. I like to read the paper, especially if Marty is still asleep. I linger in a way that I don't recall in the past. My favorite thing, routinely, is sitting on the patio with a book or this journal or a phone call.

Our patio is one of my greatest joys. I am mad about the birds. Little yellow finches, fat doves, long-tailed somethings with a sweet song. They make me happy. I love the shade patterns and the way the cushions feel on my back. The side garden, the "English Garden," has been generous with roses and Meyer lemons. (I made a pie!) The flagstone crumbles in a way that feels more natural than destructive. A giving way. The lavender and nasturtiums are full of bees. Hope and sweetness. Out front, the ice plant is flush with color—screaming pinks and magentas and everything in between. The red in the crown of thorns clashes without offense. All the cactus stand constant. When the colors fade, they will be their same selves. All of it, desert, delicate, tropical is a delight.

I feel such gratitude to be in this little house at this big time.

It's easy to not notice that 50,000 people have died in the U.S. now, the Congress has passed a $484 billion dollar coronavirus relief bill for small businesses and hospitals and the state has waived the fee requirement on usable bags.

Day 43: April 26, 2020

They are opening the ocean tomorrow. What an odd and welcome announcement. That magnificent healing body has been forbidden for these weeks. The fear of closeness in contrast to the vast space is absurd but real. Meantime, the ocean and sky and land and animals have taken this human recess to restore themselves. The lesson is profound if we're willing to learn. Write this down...People gone/Earth heals.

The part we haven't begun to consider is what happens next. This isn't "The boys come home from war and the boom begins." This crisis has revealed us—as individuals, as leaders, as communities, as countries. We are quite remarkable in some of those roles and nothing short of moronic in others. This is the week that the President of the United States asked if there was merit to injecting bleach. And yet, as I write that, I am terrified that it won't undo him because nothing else has and his transgressions have been lethal. This was the week that a nurse stood in front of a convoy of protesters who were intent on disruption. They were angry at the restrictions that the Colorado governor had placed on the state. "Land of the Free" signs were met by hospital workers who have been fighting on the COVID frontline for weeks. A quiet man in scrubs stopped the parade and, in a Tiananmen Square moment, defined the next chapter. A brand new us vs. them.

This was also the week that our neighbors exchanged sweet greetings through masks and, six feet apart, stretched and breathed in the little exercise circle at the cul-de-sac led by a kind young man, Richard, whose work-out business is slack. This is the week when Marty and I shared cafe sandwiches on the patio with Marilyn, Chinese food with Susan and Jon, Italian dinner with Natalie and Bill, each time taking such care and measured distance. Air kisses, no hugs. Separate eating trays and serving spoons and salt and pepper. And then, always, that short conversation about how good that felt and self-assurance that we were careful and all is well. Right? I'm sure we're okay. We're fine. Right?

We had FaceTime with J.T., Kate and Mirabel. Those conversations fill me up! Mirabel was holding a picture of me and saying, "Mammy." Only thing better would be to squeeze her close and say, "Yes, Angel. What is it?" She would take one finger of my hand, because that's what fits right now, and we would head wherever her heart wants to go. Soon. Please, God. They were planning a drive into Manhattan to take in the strangeness and to gather wine. A worthy and curious Sunday drive.

I am going to do the Sunday Jumble. A challenge but after a visit with Mirabel, I am up to the task.

Day 45: April 28, 2020

Our pandemic pup is driving us nuts!

Poppy is still cuter than cute but has more energy than three toddlers on a rampage. Forget the lab we thought we had adopted. This dog is pure hound—probably beagle without the colors. She has two gears—fast and stopped, one passion—digging, and an appetite that would shame a high school football captain.

So, she is off to boot camp. Jessica, our wonderful trainer, happens to be a little more available than usual since she usually trains dogs in groups. We seized on her free time and she's giving Poppy her best shot. A modified howl and a few understood commands would go a long way.

Meanwhile, children in Spain under the age of fourteen were allowed outside today for the first time in six weeks.

Day 47: April 30, 2020

Alice and Robin are finally back home in England. Our longtime friends have made San Diego their second home since their youngest moved here years ago. If plans had stayed in place, they would have enjoyed a long month of visiting and headed back to the UK but plans, as we know, didn't factor into COVID. They've been trying to get home since mid-March but lock-downs, visa issues and life kept getting in the way.

Alice posted ghostly images of the trip. Empty terminal at LAX, closed shops, near-vacant airplane. They masked up and appreciated the kind crew who had just gotten the news that they would be laid off. Alice had taken boxes of chocolates to blunt the pain for all of them, a small but worthy salve. They'll be home, quarantined, for two weeks and then can restock the fridge. Meantime, as we all are, they'll be at the mercy of friends and neighbors.

I sent my DIL, Kate, a silly gift and she's made good use of it—a batch of small rocks and a set of paint pens for decorating them. She's clever with a pen and put sweet images on them. Some were lessons for Mirabel—cow, duck, cat. Others had rainbows and hearts and the word "vecinos" or "amigo." These she tossed over the fence of Puerto Rican neighbors and friends. She seemed pleased for the artistic respite.

California Governor Gavin Newsom has announced that, beginning tomorrow, the state's beaches and parks will close again. Evidently, we can't get this social distancing thing quite right.

May 2020

"Aren't you worried?"
"Would that help?"'

~Bridge of Spies

Day 48: May 1, 2020

I have the smallest inkling of what a drug deal might feel like. This morning, I went to a nearby parking lot off the alley behind the shop. I sat in the car, fully masked. I phoned inside to say, "I'm here." A few moments later, Larry was standing, at a distance, beside my window where I passed him fifty dollars cash and he handed me the brown paper bag.

Inside, I found two tubes of hair coloring, a clip, comb, plastic gloves and instructions.

After tonight, the gray will be gone.

Day 49: May 2, 2020

Our kids had a family photo taken this week. By a professional. It's a precious picture of a devoted, happy mother, an affectionate father and pigtailed child playing beside a flower box in their back yard. All the sweet closeness oozes through the picture even though the photographer wasn't there. It was all managed remotely. He gave direction to J.T. and Kate about where and how to set the camera on their phone. Click. Change positions. Click. Repeat. We are learning new ways.

J.T. and Kate are working so hard right now but at least they're working and the news keeps reminding them that they're among the lucky ones. The Labor Department reported that thirty million claims were made for unemployment in the last six weeks and that number may be low. States are reportedly so overwhelmed with claims, they can't verify the correctness of their numbers. COVID has shut down many workplaces and the pain and panic is real for thousands.

Meantime, Trump is playing to the lowest common denominator, mocking the "CHIII-NA" origins of the virus and suggesting that he will extract a financial compensation from that country.

It's just plain embarrassing.

Day 51: May 4, 2020

We are still sheltered in place. Mostly. There's not a lot of incentive to venture out when the death toll for the United States just reached 63,000. In the world, the number has exceeded 3.26 million according to Johns Hopkins University. Still, some perspective is needed. Against the 233,000 deaths, they also report more than one million recoveries. That counts.

Day 53: May 6, 2020

Mine was the only car in the parking lot at the beach this morning. The posted signs read, "No stopping. No sitting. Keep 6-foot social distance." At the beach. I walked to my pier and walked back. No stopping. No sitting. Sigh.

Day 57: May 10, 2020

Life is shifting slightly—like a dune. The movement is constant but the experience gives a sense that nothing has changed and the result is a constant disorientation. Wasn't I just here? Which day was that? Who did I say that to? Who told me that story? Was that just a month ago? Has it already been two months?

It's all been a gateway for folks who are inclined to depression. I'm grateful that I have dodged that. I've been down or lonely at times in my life, but the chronic condition of hopelessness is a curse I've been spared. That's not true for some of the people I love though, so I know a little about the anxiety and malaise that are part of depression. This condition—this pandemic of global proportions—brings with it so many of those same descriptors: confusion, sadness, loneliness. If you add those to genuine clinical depression, I can't imagine the pain that some are feeling and how hard it must be to cope.

I haven't written as much lately and I'm not sure why or what I have done instead. That's one of the strange commonalities of this time. We all seem to be chronically stalled. Many Zoom meetings sharing many thoughts with many people who think like us and are all experiencing all of this in a common way.

What are you doing? Not much.

What do you miss? Hugs. Friends.

What are you reading? *Where the Crawdads Sing. A Promised Land.*

What could we do to help others? Stall. That damn age thing or risk factor thing or, honestly, inertia thing, blocks the path.

Before this roadblock, I was one of the helpers. Not officially like a nurse or teacher or fireman but I was quick to reach out or find a cause that I cared about to try to make things better. That was true for my friends, too. We grew up with the same mantra—if you're not part of the solution, you're part of the problem. But now, as the older, at-risk crowd, our contribution is to stay out of the way. Seems like a small ask, but it feels like an insult and it doesn't sit well.

It's Mother's Day today and I got the best gift—FaceTime with J.T., Kate and Mirabel this morning. Gawd, that child is magic. She knows the power she wields, even on the screen and she works it! Her vocabulary is accelerating at warp speed. Her language, like everything about her, dazzles me. I am in awe of the three of them and how they have coped. For all of the strain they feel, it doesn't show when we talk. J.T. and Kate's love seems to have deepened and their devotion to their daughter is boundless. I miss them all terribly, but I know they are safe and loving each other so, for now, all is well.

Or well enough.

Day 61: May 14, 2020

I'm sitting upstairs while the housekeepers clean my puppy-hair coated house. Their help is a great privilege that comes with equal portions of guilt and gratitude.

The ups and downs of this time are colliding with "does anybody really know what's going on?" It's clear that this virus is not leaving soon and the longer it stays, the wider the circles of damage. New York just announced that all subways will be shut down indefinitely. California universities are not planning an in-person fall session. Broadway has cancelled all production until at least September.

The show must not go on.

Are we being too cautious or not cautious enough?

Our "normal"—the one that Marty and I share—is finding its own shape. Sitting, at some distance, with friends on the patio, is normal now. And precious. We know there are rules and we're doing our best to follow them. We're adjusting to the awkwardness of the demands. Separate platters, serve yourself cocktails, blankets for the chillier evenings when we would otherwise have gone inside. Not now. Curiously, the conversation is almost all COVID. We are fascinated and owned by it. We can talk about friends, films, family. But it always comes back to the pandemic, the virus in the middle of the room.

Most of the time our normal is just us and the pup. Two older people who can't wait for the next episode of *Schitt's Creek*, which we'll watch from the sofa holding hands when we're not eating ice cream. It's a normal that, right now, does not include worries about children or illness or financial challenges and I should be slapped, hard, if I find a reason to complain.

Day 62: May 15, 2020

Message on a neighborhood sandwich board: "Right about now, many parents are discovering that the teacher wasn't the problem."

Day 63: May 16, 2020

A pause for the trivial. I have gained five pounds in these sixty-three days which makes me about fifteen pounds fatter than I would like to be. This is a moment of "be very careful what you wish for" to be sure, but it may also be a time to insert a bit of self-discipline into self-quarantine. I know how lucky I am for the quality of life and limited stress in my version of sheltering, but I also recognize an inclination to give in to pleasures just because everything is so shitty. Dishes in the sink longer than usual. TV shows of limited quality and less limited quantity. Laundry delayed. Ice cream at night. Every night. And a bowl of popcorn most afternoons along with three square meals. I've done a hell of a lot of cooking in the last two months with only a half-mind toward calorie count. Those veggies did not want for olive oil.

Eating habits and nutrition will be an interesting thread to follow in the months ahead. Since March, pizza chains are growing. Pizza Hut added 30,000 new employees. The food section of the paper devotes time every week to healthy choices during the pandemic. "Easy, affordable" menus really aren't if you're a stressed parent or budget anxious family. Lots of fruits and vegetables means shopping and preparing. McDonald's drive-thru is an oasis. "Processed foods" is a big topic of what not to do but we all know that hot dogs and beans are in the basic food group for the apocalyptic table. The old weight joke for college kids— Freshman 15—has been updated to COVID 19.

Some would argue that it's a time of self-nurturing and we're worrying about all the wrong stuff, but the fact remains, obesity is one of the greatest risk factors for COVID and many other diseases. We are getting fatter, and we will pay that price as a nation. One more condition exacerbated in this time.

Never mind the nation. What about me? Personal change happens at the point of sufficient disgust. Am I sufficiently disgusted? Honestly, disgust overstates it. There's no self-loathing in me but maybe I could be almost-disgusted enough to make the weeks ahead count for the good of Gail. Bring my best self and end up with a little less of me.

As my seventieth birthday approaches, I will make the same wish I made coming into my fiftieth and sixtieth. "May I look good in a great white shirt tucked into a pair of jeans." I'll be seventy for a whole year so let me add to that, "May that great white shirt have my granddaughter's fingerprints all over it!"

Day 66: May 19, 2020

I didn't watch the news today—a healthier choice but not one I can sustain. I'm a junkie. Always was even when news was impartial and brief and produced only by old white men.

A friend came for lunch. She's a junkie, too, so we can never veer far from news and politics. We've been through a few administrations together and we both long for one that is dominated by common sense and decency and, honestly, women. We talked about the VP part of the ticket. Amy or Kamala or Stacy? (Speaking of them by first names—proof of affection or lingering sexism? "Mr. Jones and his secretary, Sue.") My friend is smart and funny and full of fire. This stillness is hard for her after a lifetime with a partner who matched her passion. He died a few years ago but she soldiers on and there are few whom I admire more.

Another topic for us today: the president has decided to take (or have us think that he's taking) hydroxychloroquine. Long story but, for now, let me just enter into the record another example of what an idiot this man is. The chapters that will be written about him, and there will be quantities that could fill a local library, will focus on his greed, his malevolence, his damage, and his abuse of power. They won't begin to tell the whole story or do justice to how it felt to live through his time in power.

I don't want to end a day with that story so I will say that I made another dandy dinner. Healthy, balanced, and tasty. I even used herbs. When I was in school, I never admitted that I was a competent typist for fear of being tasked with the job whenever someone needed a term paper typed. Cooking was always that way, too. If you say you're no good, nobody asks you to do it. But now I'm afraid I've doomed myself. At almost seventy, even I know that I'm a damn fine cook and now I'm probably stuck in the kitchen.

Another casualty of COVID. Damn virus.

Day 70: May 23, 2020

We're opening up! That's the report from pretty much everybody and pretty much nobody knows what the hell that means.

Literally, it means restaurants and shops that have been shuttered for weeks can ditch the takeout table blocking the door and fling those doors open. They can, finally, let in 25% of the crowds and couples desperate for Phase Two. So far, so good. Waiters in masks, hand sanitizer throughout, disposable menus. Tables are spaced apart, some marked with an "X" or removed altogether. Creative placement of mannequins or stuffed animals or even plants. Plexiglass walls installed to partition diners. "There is a great future in plastics. Think about it. Will you think about it?" The Graduate meets George Orwell.

Phase Two. As one pundit said, "It doesn't mean the virus is gone. It means that there's room for you in the ICU." Dark but real. But dark.

COVID stats are still grim. Globally, as of today, 5.2 million cases and 338,000 deaths reported. But who thinks globally? Fact is, no one in my neighborhood is sick, as far as I know. Brazil is digging mass graves, but my world is full of people on bikes, walking their dogs, and, maybe, dining out. Most of them wear masks. It all looks fine, right? We can't know which ones have lost their jobs or their grandmother or their patience. Which ones are suffering from depression or struggling with their children's schoolwork or waking up with a cough and feeling a panic. With or without a mask, we have all lived behind a quiet plexiglass partition of our own for nearly three months.

Phase Two brings our country's division into sharp relief. As a nation, we are so broken. I blame Trump and his minions, but the media has hurt us too. Our prisms are forever altered by the last two presidencies. Us vs. Them. Red vs. Blue. Rednecks vs. Libs. Today's headlines reflect that prism. MSNBC: "Trump wants houses of worship reopened as U.S. deaths near 100,000." (His press secretary suggested that the press didn't believe in God.) Fox headline: "Under fire, Cuomo tries to deflect NY's deadly nursing home debacle onto Trump." Blame game on steroids from both sides.

So, here we are. Phase Two. Our measured gatherings with friends are still filled with talk about the pandemic but now we talk about what to do going forward. Take our chances with baby steps? Let the non-mask wearers take the hit to get us to herd immunity? Is that even possible? Stay behind our doors and off our airplanes and away from our restaurants so we're safe? *Twilight Zone* episodes were based on that notion. Once again, I think of my mother's resolve not to be on the apocalyptic cleanup committee—no bomb shelter for her. As we try to get our bearings, science and human nature promise there will be another wave. And another. And another.

Supreme Court Chief Justice John Roberts gave a virtual graduation address yesterday and spoke about the pandemic. He told the seniors that they may meet people who "bear scars you may not see." He told them to practice humility, adding that the "pandemic should teach us at least that."

I would like us to add the lesson of kindness. Humility and kindness. We don't know each others paths or fears or scars. In this phase, let kindness and humility be as viral as the pandemic.

June 2020

"But then again, maybe bad things happen because it's the only way we can keep remembering what good is supposed to look like."

~Jodi Picoult

Day 97: June 19, 2020

Had time truly stopped or stalled, then there would be little to tell by the gap of entries from the last twenty-eight days. But we are in strange times and there are many reasons I have not been writing. "Nothing to tell" is not one of them.

In this short time:

- I fell and made a crash landing on my elbow that caused two bone breaks requiring major surgery, two pins, a wire loop, and a daunting cast. Marty could not be with me for the exam or the surgery or the hospital overnight. COVID rules. The hospital was eerie and quiet and the nurses' eyes told the stories of exhaustion and strain. In eight weeks I can pick up Mirabel— if I can see Mirabel. For now, I can't lift more than a cup of coffee and I'm lousy on the keyboard.

- George Floyd, a forty-six-year-old black man, was killed by a police officer who knelt on his neck for 8:46 minutes while three other officers stood by. They believed he had tried to pass a counterfeit twenty dollar bill. His last words were cries for his mother.

- Demonstrations, some of them violent, organized in every major city, including San Diego. Here, two banks were burned down and windows downtown were smashed. Small shit compared to destruction in New York, Minneapolis, Pittsburg.

- Hundreds of thousands of people began marching for Black Lives Matter. The right said that all lives matter and the left became exhausted trying to explain the distinction.

- I turned seventy on pain meds and had a parade of friends outside and a Zoom party at the computer. I sort of remember them both.

- The Coronavirus Task Force seemed to lose interest and briefings stopped.

- The President cleared protesters with force and walked to a church and held a Bible upside-down and walked back.

- Our puppy, Poppy, found a forever home with more room, more kids and more adoration. The broken arm was the final act that showed us that this sweet pup deserved a bustling home. Ours is many things, but bustling it is not. We get frequent pictures from her new owner showing Poppy playing with the children, taking long walks with the mistress, and getting boiled chicken for her dinner. Poppy will be just fine and so will we.
- A house finch made a nest outside the front door and laid five eggs. They are beginning to hatch.
- Mirabel said many sentences that only she completely understands.
- Albertsons, Vons, Target, and Trader Joe's continued their special senior hours but haven't figured out how to handle those young people who don't care about the rules.
- We decided to drive to New York. And then decided not to. And then changed our minds again. And changed them again.
- Two more generals issued strong statements questioning Trump's judgment.
- Cars all over town were painted up with cheers for a graduate who didn't get to walk in June. Horns are the new "Pomp and Circumstance."
- We participated in a Black Lives Matter demonstration down Sixth Avenue. Ours was more observation than movement, but loud cheering prevailed and I raised my good arm.
- Joe Biden announced that he will run for president.
- I got my hair cut and professionally colored for the first time in three months.
- And the U.S. reached 2.28 million cases of COVID with 121,000 deaths. New York and California remain #1 and #2 in highest numbers.

Those are the broad strokes—the national ones that might make it into the history books and the personal ones that have made up my life. Four short head-spinning weeks.

Day 98: June 20, 2020

2020 will be a defining year for us all. It's as if 1918 and 1968 had a not-so-loved child. We've been here before, but it's entirely unrecognizable and our White Board shows eraser marks of a lesson's faint remains. But it's gone now.

Trump will hold his first rally tonight with claims that over one million people requested a ticket. In fact, 19,000 will attend if it reaches full capacity—bumper to bumper bums. No face masks required in Oklahoma, which has one of the fastest COVID infection rates in the country. A barn burner and a super spreader. A near certain outcome. He has escalated his hateful rhetoric just as John Bolton's book, *The Room Where it Happened*, is released detailing the president's vile behavior. "It's all a lie, a lie!" Trump shouts. "He's disclosed top security information." Both can't be true, but that's the world we're navigating right now.

Time, which has always passed quickly for me, moves at lightning speed right now. Others comment on it, too. We don't know why. Perhaps this strange chapter gives a warped sense of warp speed. Sunday shows up sooner every week.

When I broke my elbow, my blog went dormant for a few weeks, a combination of distraction and an inability to type. I did have one inspired moment six days in and dictated:

Day 6 since the elbow smack down. My hands are becoming good partners with increased empathy for each other. This morning my left hand insisted on putting in my contacts without assistance. My right hand was very proud. No ego in them. I think they will be glad to resume their roles as primary and support. But it shows, through this time, we are all learning how to make it work.

Day 108: June 30, 2020

COVID has killed 500,000 people. 125,000 have been in the United States.

That's the AP headline with a report of more than ten million cases. Florida is closing its beaches again. LA is closing its bars.

It's back.

July 2020

"If you don't like something, change it.
If you can't change it, change your attitude."

~Maya Angelou

Day 111: July 3, 2020

My elbow mends as the country splits apart. We're beginning to hear the word "fascism" a lot. Last night it was repeated at Mount Rushmore, where Trump gave a dark, divisive speech to an anticipated massive crowd. But here's the rub: the million-person Trump rally that could only seat 19,000 yielded just 6,500 attendees. Blame was assigned to protesters, traffic, fear of the virus, media, but, in fact, it was mostly a lot of young people who ordered tickets they would never use. Clever kids!

Trump used the moment for a Blue Angels fly-over and fireworks to sow more division. All the talk about the millions that were reached on TV would not assuage him after this diminished crowd. He's a master of race baiting: "Angry mobs are trying to tear down statues of our founders, deface our most sacred memorials and unleash a wave of violent crime in our cities," and intensified darkness: "Our nation is witnessing a merciless campaign to wipe out our history, defame our heroes, erase our values and indoctrinate our children." Biden is surging in the polls and we're afraid to believe it and afraid not to. There are four months until the election which we must win but, if we do, it will come at a cost and the split will surely become a chasm.

COVID has spiked to more than 50,000 cases a day in the United States for several days now. Total cases have reached 2.8 million with almost 130,000 related deaths. Europe, among others, will not allow U.S. visitors. Restaurants that had reopened are re-closing. Nobody quite knows what "back to normal" is. How far back? Which normal?

The simple joys have never been so important. Lunch or dinner on the patio with one or two friends. Monday night happy hour Zoom with the high school lifelong pals (even as we feel political strain increasing), cock-and-walks (walking with a cocktail) in the neighborhood, a few more episodes of *Schitt's Creek*.

But some occasions demand a bigger effort and a little inventive risk taking. *The Orange Woods*, an enchanting memoir written by my friend Marilyn, is now in print and, pandemic be damned, must be launched. In other times, Marilyn would be on the writer's circuit with talks at bookstores, with signings and hugs. But these are not those times.

So we find new ways to celebrate. When this is over, these adaptations will probably be dropped as fast as a mutant cat tied to a rock sinks in a river, but for now we marvel at our creative COVID end-runs. *The Orange Woods* was officially launched on our patio with fourteen friends seated an imperfect four-to-six-foot distance from each other. The invitation promised: "We will be socially close and physically distant with special care given to everyone's safety and delight."

Guests were ushered straight to their assigned seat marked by their name on an orange-tissued goodie bag. Lunch was on orange trays with champagne and orange seltzer water. The guest list was composed of smart and loving women and an honoree who brought full animation to the adoring crowd. She read. She explained. She elaborated. The gods showed up to give us a perfect sunny afternoon. Orange, the color and the fruit, is a versatile, fragrant and delicious theme.

Improvisation at its best. It was an altogether satisfying and happy afternoon.

New rules are better than ruled out.

Day 112: July 4, 2020

It's the Fourth of July in COVID land.

Forty years ago this week, I arrived in Washington, D.C. as a new bride. I left my folks, my job, my friends, my home, and started a grand adventure on Capitol Hill.

It was a stiflingly hot night on my first July fourth in D.C. We lived seven blocks from the Capitol, and I had been a resident for two days. (Our wedding was on the 28th, a party with his parents in Los Angeles on the 29th, Las Vegas on the 30th and 1st, D.C. on the 2nd.) Marty, on a split shift, met me on the Washington Mall for a quick picnic before he returned to anchor the 11 o'clock news. He headed back to cover what would surely be firecracker accidents and traffic jams. I stayed on "The Hill" to hear the Marine Corps band and The Beach Boys.

It was not a big crowd—just locals in the middle of the week—and I sat on the Capitol steps in my denim cut-offs and striped red tank top. The Corps was magnificent. They completely overcame their horrible heavy uniforms and made freedom ring. The Beach Boys, luckier in their Hawaiian shirts, were past their "Best by…" date but still, it was the Beach Boys. A few fireworks later I walked home, locked the door, and waited for Marty's 11:45 return home. I was at once hot, sweaty, a little anxious and awestruck.

I will always be grateful for the experiences and friendships of the two-and-a-half years that followed. A time of learning and growing, a time of celebrity and importance (real or perceived), jam-packed with experiences that have shaped me—and us.

On our anniversary last Sunday, Marty gave me a small ruby pendant—the fortieth anniversary gem. Red—the color of fire and celebration. Of love and blood and depth and mystery. The rarest gem. Like Marty. We have survived and suffered and thrived through so much and have settled into a quiet sharing that suits us. Still compatible in a pandemic. Good to know.

Barring the worst, some of us—the lucky ones—may look back at this time with a bit of longing and affection. Forced solitude can be quite comfy. I believe and hope we will take some of these lessons forward, and that would be a good thing. I hope I can remember that stillness is rich, gratitude is essential, and love can be very quiet.

The New York Times reports that COVID cases are rising in thirty-six states with California, Arizona, Texas, and Florida all posting record numbers of new infections this week.

Today we will celebrate the Fourth of July, 2020, with Ann and Terry—our very first friends in Washington, D.C. that summer of

1980. We will grill burgers and whine about Trump and remember other Fourths that included a crowded beach and noisy children, bottle rockets, sparklers, and roman candles. We'll toast freedom and independence as we know it and say a prayer that it will prevail in 2021.

Day 114: July 6, 2020

A sign in the window of a nearby restaurant:

"To accommodate ANTI-MASKERS, we have provided a space 40 feet west where you can stare at your reflection in the window since apparently you're the only person you care about."

Day 115: July 7, 2020

The headline of today's *Union-Tribune*: San Diego Hospitalizations Tie Single Day Record. The "More Coverage Inside" teased three more articles: (1) Churches become virus spreaders as services resume, (2) Lawsuit claims region not helping disabled homeless people and (3) Jorge Mateo becomes the second Padre to test Positive.

Day 118: July 10, 2020

It's Friday. I miss the San Diego Symphony POPS this summer. Our first year in many without the magical Friday night on the bay with the sounds of a full orchestra, a little buzz from mediocre wine, and the smell of ocean air. Sharing hugs with special friends and holding hands with my honey while the music washes over us. My very favorite grown-up thing to do in San Diego. But not this year.

Day 120: July 12, 2020

There's a new element to litter now. Besides the cigarette butts and trash wrappers, discarded masks are everywhere. Mostly the blue and white ones but black or fabric or shiny versions are part of the clutter, too. I started taking pictures of them but it feels like photographing dead bugs and I quit.

Day 123: July 15, 2020

Supreme Court Justice Ruth Bader Ginzburg has been hospitalized. She's 87 and has survived cancer a few times but losing her could send things south in a big way.

And Jeff Sessions lost his Alabama Senate Race to Tommy Tuberville. A college football coach is a senator now because the former Attorney General made Trump mad.

And Mirabel played with baby goats in her other grandmother's neighborhood in upstate New York. It's important to remember what matters.

Day 124: July 16, 2020

I just figured out there have been more days of the pandemic than there are days left before the election. I wish that prompted more joy.

Are there stages of grief in a global crisis? I think there are for me. Or maybe they are just recurring cycles. I'm in a *malaise* stage. "A general feeling of illness or discomfort whose exact cause is difficult to identify," says the dictionary. The exact cause, COVID, is universal, of course, but my own experience is harder to define and, therefore, overcome. I just feel sad. Sad for personal reasons and sad for the trouble I see coming at us. Sad for my country and my kids.

San Diego is back in just-before-lockdown-mode again. Restaurants have closed, beauty salons, parks. People got too close, too confident, too stupid. Mostly, our national nature is being revealed and it's not pretty. We have rants from those demanding independence: "You're violating my civil rights!" and "They don't work!" answered with shouts from those with good sense: "Just wear the fucking mask!"

We were supposed to be in Oregon right now. Long drive up and back with a scenic change and a lot of loving laughter with friends who know everything about us. We were supposed to see their new town and make new memories there. We were supposed to have some fun. "Supposed to…" comes up a lot these days. So does "not supposed to…" We weren't supposed to go to the urgent care to see if Marty's fall on July fifth was a shoulder bruise or a break. We weren't supposed to make the trip with just one person able to drive. We're not supposed to be surprised when things get cancelled anymore.

We're learning to just go with it even when we don't go at all.

I drove up to Orange County to see my eighty-nine-year-old Aunt Donna yesterday and we had a wonderful visit. She's dear to many of us and it's unfair that one of her final chapters is being written in relative isolation. I'm grateful that she has all the creature comforts of a lovely apartment, some outdoor space, friends who call, and family who loves her. I think of the millions for whom this isolation is far worse. Physically, emotionally, mentally.

An assault of loneliness.

Day 126: July 18, 2020

Our neighborhood is all about games lately. Hop-scotch everywhere, playfully outlined in chalk on the sidewalks. Chalk drawings with messages like, "The time is always right to do what is right," written with pastels and bright suns and double wording. "Thank you Essential Warriors" and "Warrors (sic) are not the ones who always win but the ones who always fight." Houses with rocks out front invite us to balance them and the result is rows of artistically stacked stones, some quite high. We all seek quiet moments of play.

And then, the not-playing-games part of our neighborhood. Every business door with the clutter of signs explaining the rules, mapping the sanitary lotion dispensers and demanding a mask.

Mirabel's playing games in New York. Her folks bought her a potty seat. She likes to wear it as a hat or hold up the seat and look through it like a picture frame. Her newest word is "hug" which is always in the form of a question. I can't wait for my chance.

Day 132: July 24, 2020

We've hit another milestone. The U.S. has had four million confirmed cases of COVID. On July 7th, it was three. June 10th it was two. There's a pattern here and it's alarming.

Last week, at a safe distance and after cancelling a bigger gathering, we celebrated Alicia's seventieth. Just four girlfriends, wearing our masks, playing bocce ball, sitting apart with separately plated appetizers, individually boxed dinners. Even with all these limitations, it was a joyful celebration and we, as cultured ladies often do, laughed our asses off.

Day 133: July 25, 2020

Gotta admit, I've had some blue days lately. I don't want to ignore those moments, but I also don't want to dwell on them. It's hard to shake it off, though.

Today's headlines, for example:
- Portland is in day fifty-six of protests. Enough already but the Feds are there in uniform looking dystopian and malignant

along with the Wall of Moms in yellow shirts, Wall of Dads with leaf blowers, Wall of Vets who are just pissed at the whole thing.

- ◆ Congressman and Civil Rights leader John Lewis is being eulogized. Lewis led the march from Selma to Montgomery in 1965 and endured vicious beatings. The images from that time galvanized support for the Voting Rights Act. He was a true champion of good trouble.
- ◆ Almost 144,000 have died of COVID in the U.S.
- ◆ There are one hundred days until the Presidential election. Biden is favored in the polls and the only thing we know with certainty is that anything could happen.
- ◆ Yosemite has tested positive for COVID. What? Water samples don't lie.
- ◆ The San Diego Padres won their first game. It'll be a weird, crowd-less, short season, but the Pads won. Something.

Day 134: July 26, 2020

Tonight I went in to Rubio's—a fast food taco shop—to pick up dinner. The dining area was closed off with four tables. One each for Doordash, UberEats, Grubhub, and Express Pick-up. Mine was there. Hot doesn't matter nearly as much as safe these days.

Day 136: July 28, 2020

The kids sent a video of Mirabel watching the ice cream truck go by. She wiggles her little butt to the music and waves and dances a little more. To her, at nineteen months, the ice cream truck is just a wonderful music machine. No need to know that there's something magical inside. The gift of music is enough.

August 2020

"Today was good. Today was fun. Tomorrow is another one."

~Dr. Seuss

Day 140: August 1, 2020

We had a wonderful Zoom visit with our friends, John and Karen, today. That friendship of forty years is still one of our dearest. Our politics are not entirely in sync, but our conversations are thoughtful and respectful. Karen has always called me "honey." I think she calls many people "honey," but it feels like it's just me and I love it. John is the conservative I trust the most to exchange ideas and give it a fair shot. And we all agree that this president must go.

Six months ago, they were here from Florida for a visit. We saw 2019 out and toasted an exciting year ahead. It was a lovely evening. Nobody said, "Fasten your seat belt. It's gonna be a bumpy ride." Nobody said, "You thought these last three years were weird, wait'll you see this one." Nobody thought, "I sure hope we don't have a pandemic this year, or violent protests or one branch of government completely abdicate to another branch of government."

Nobody.

Adventures at our house continue. My arm is great. I've moved from range-of-motion to strength training. I'm a tough cookie, Marty says. Meanwhile, he is still feeling great shoulder pain and will try to get more answers this week. Oh, and he flew one of his remote-control planes into his face and needed twelve stitches on his nose. Could've been way worse but still... who flies a plane into their face?

Tomorrow we'll find out what our kids want to do about a visit to San Diego. I'm desperate to see them and if they decide they can't safely make the journey, I'm determined to find a way to New York. It seems everyone has an opinion about that.

"FLY! The planes are empty and their ventilation makes them super safe."

"DON'T FLY! It's the easiest way to get COVID!"

"DRIVE! You don't have to quarantine on the other side."

"DON'T DRIVE! Do you know how far that is? How many toilet stops?"

"Are you nuts? STAY PUT! This is all going to end soon. Travel then."

"BETTER DO IT NOW! Nobody knows when this thing is going to end."

You can't get a straight answer on anything anymore.

Day 141: August 2, 2020

They're coming! J.T., Kate, and Mirabel have booked a modest Airbnb in Pacific Beach. Remote work. Me as nanny. August 15 – September 13. I'm pretty sure I've died and gone to heaven.

Day 142: August 3, 2020

I've been reading about a Happiness Museum that opened recently in Copenhagen. What good timing. Its mission reads:

Our hope is that guests will leave a little wiser, a little happier and a little more motivated to make the world a better place. We all seem to be looking for happiness – but perhaps we are looking in the wrong places. We have gotten richer as societies but often failed to become happier. Therefore, the Happiness Research Institute decided to create a museum where we can bring happiness to life.

When this is over, I need to add it to my places to visit. I hope it's still open.

Day 146: August 7, 2020

It's been ferociously hot and we're facing some of the first rolling blackouts since 2001. Places where folks usually go to escape the heat—beaches or movie theaters—are closed or shuttered.

We could talk about climate change or the approaching fire season but enough already. Plus my kids will be here soon so, hands over my ears, la, la, la, la…

Day 149: August 10, 2020

More than five million people in the United States have been diagnosed with COVID now and 163,000 of them have died. Our neighbor, a youngish man in the little house behind us, was one. I never met him. Rest in peace.

Day 153: August 14, 2020

Big prep for the kids' arrival. I found a crib on FaceBook Marketplace. Picked up basic groceries (their list), paper towels, Clorox wipes, toilet paper, hand sanitizer as well as (my list) wine, cheese, ice cream, chips, berries. Checked the bedding at the rental (looks ok), delivered a few toys and planted an Elmo chair in the middle of the living room. We've been restricting our contact with anyone. Not quite quarantined but darn safe and, of course, tested.

I am so ready. So, so ready.

Day 154: August 15, 2020

We met the kids at the airport. Marty drove one car—they'll borrow that one and it includes a car seat, borrowed from a friend. I drove the other car so we won't have the nervousness of close shared space after we pick them up.

When Mirabel stepped off the elevator, I caught my breath. She's a tiny little vision. Pink gingham dress, beach hat, plexiglass shield over her face, and a pink polka-dot mask over her mouth. A miniature pandemic model who walks and talks and smiles with her eyes. We made it all the way to the curb before I could wait no longer and scooped her into my arms. She patted my cheek.

My kids are home.

Day 157: August 18, 2020

I don't know if it's the heat or a style thing but Mirabel's favorite fashion moment happens when she strips naked, slips into her mother's tennis shoes, pulls the ties up like they are handles, and wanders the apartment.

Day 159: August 20, 2020

It's hotter than hell so time with Mirabel has been all about the fifteen dollar plastic pool from Ace Hardware. The pandemic has closed the parks, libraries, and playgrounds that would normally be our haunts, so it's challenging to find adventures, but we're managing and I wouldn't trade the time for anything!

J.T. and Kate have virtually burrowed into their work with a few evening social hours that consist of sitting on the front lawn of their rental or taking the four-block walk to put toes in the sand and bodies in the sea. I think they're glad to be here.

The universities in San Diego have reopened, sort of. In a town usually short on student housing, *The San Diego Union/Tribune* reports over 13,300 empty beds at the five campuses. In a town usually teaming with returning students, a stillness haunts all the campuses as most students will return for virtual learning only. In a town that counts the universities as a primary industry, the pandemic has cost those campuses $492 million so far. It's too soon to measure the cost to the college kids.

Day 161: August 22, 2020

In case you needed more proof that America is going off the rails, today President Trump praised followers of QAnon. This far right conspiracy group dates back to October of 2017. At its core, it's a theory about Trump saving the world from pedophiles, cannibals, and satanic worshippers.

"Is that a bad thing?" he asked when told about the group. The FBI has labeled QAnon as a domestic terrorist threat but that doesn't stop the president from encouraging them. "So, I don't know really anything about it other than they do supposedly like me."

According to NPR, research from the liberal watchdog group Media Matters for America counts twenty candidates for Congress who will appear on the general election ballot in November that have either identified themselves as believers in QAnon or have given credence to its dogma.

Twenty!

Day 163: August 24, 2020

I've been pretty obsessed with the election and have been reporting those efforts on FaceBook. Today's entry:

We have 70 days to go before election day and it's still anybody's guess. I've gotten on what my dad would call my "high horse" a few times (he would have been up there with me) but I'm going to try to be a little less angry—a little more kind and hopeful. I've written postcards, made calls, bought stamps, called friends, written more postcards—and there's more of all of that to come. What are you doing?

I posted a picture of my beguiling Mirabel and said she was my inspiration. "What's yours?" I asked and got sixty-four responses, many of them with their grandchild's photo. That's what this time is for so many of us. What do we leave our children if we don't put up a fight with what seems to be assured chaos?

It's the third night of the virtual Democratic convention. Kamala Harris has been nominated for Vice-President. A woman. A black woman. A brilliant black woman. Her speech praised Biden as a man with the "vision of our nation as a beloved community—where all are welcome, no matter what we look like, where we come from, or who we love."

Hillary also spoke tonight and everyone watching must have been thinking—if only.

"For four years, people have said to me, 'I didn't realize how dangerous he was,'" Clinton said. "Well, this can't be another woulda, coulda, shoulda election."

It can't be.

September 2020

"I've developed a new philosophy.
I only dread one day at at time."

~Charlie Brown

Day 173: Sept 3, 2020

The Forbes list is out and MacKenzie Scott—novelist, philanthropist, and ex-wife of Amazon founder Jeff Bezos—is officially the third wealthiest woman in the world and the thirty-fifth wealthiest individual. She's fifty three years old and worth sixty eight billion dollars. . . a number I can't conceive even if they gave me one of those "if you linked $100 bills and made a chain to the Milky Way galaxy..." sort of illustrations.

The best news is that she is, from all reports, a kind, caring woman who sees the world as a place where she can make a significant difference. Very wealthy women are stepping up in ways that will be transformational. Melinda Gates is working with seventy billion dollars. Her focus is on education and children's health. Priscilla Chan runs the Chan Zuckerberg Initiative, giving hundreds of millions away and working with other philanthropies to create best practices. These women became wealthy through marriage but they are taking a leadership role in philanthropy that is changing the face and the approach to giving. It all makes me pretty certain that if women ruled the world, the world would look a fair site better in oh-so-many ways.

Mirabel is still busy ruling my world. We have resurrected the stuffed animals from her father's childhood and a few from mine. She lines them up, along with some that she's accumulated here, and we all make a parade. Or she piles them into a box and takes them to the (imaginary) grocery store. Sometimes she feeds them imaginary food and gives them imaginary drinks and all these things, which every child has done forever, have never been done with quite as much flair as they're done by my Mirabel.

Day 176: September 6, 2020

Los Angeles County reached its all-time hottest temperature today: 121 degrees out in Woodland Hills. Meanwhile, California wildfires have burned 2.1 million acres so far this year and not officially fire season yet. Makes me wonder if we're worrying about all the wrong stuff.

Day 178: September 8, 2020

We managed a trip to the zoo with our kids. Masks are still required. I wonder if the animals feel any distress about not seeing the face of the folks seeing them. Mirabel spent most of the visit on her daddy's shoulders and took the greatest liking to the giraffes. Me, too. They are majestic and special.

Our San Diego Zoo, the most visited zoo in the world, closed on March 16th. Before that, it had never been closed for more than a day and that had only happened five times. They reopened in the middle of June, but the masks are still required to protect us and the animals. We're beginning to understand that these beautiful creatures may not be immune to COVID, beginning with reports from the Bronx Zoo where lions and tigers have tested positive.

Day 180: September 10, 2020

One of the few encouraging things about COVID-19, we thought, was that children were not at risk. That notion has been chipped away for some months now, and a new report by the American Academy of Pediatrics and Children's Hospital Association blows that assurance sky high. The number of cases has now surpassed half a million. Severe illness does not seem to be common but it all still sets the fretting in motion.

Years ago, when I took my mom's ashes to Cripple Creek, Colorado, to rest by my dad's, I was struck by how many small shingle-like markers stood on gravesites spread over the Mt. Pisgah hillside. The weather had stolen nearly all the inscriptions but my family knew what they were. They marked the graves of the little children who had died in the 1918 flu epidemic. It was chilling then. It's more chilling now.

Day 184: September 14, 2020

Kate, J.T., and Mirabel went back to New York yesterday morning. We had nearly a whole month. It was glorious! She is a magical child, and I treasured every moment. I am officially and lovingly known as "Mimi." Marty is "Gra-pa" which is usually said before a command, as in "Gra—pa, watch Elmo!" or "Gra—pa, come!" While the kids set up camp in Pacific Beach, we shuttled back and forth to alternately drink Mirabel in and recover from her joyful energy. She is sweet, smart, and funny as hell.

Our son and daughter-in-law are hard workers. I admire the commitment and work ethic they bring to this contrived time. I hope they're set free from it soon, but they are making it work for now. They gathered with friends while they were here but with strict limitations of "bring your own lawn chair and beer." Their visit, clearly, was mostly for us. For four lovely weeks we got to be local grandparents. I babysat and we played chase. I made breakfast (sometimes), lunch and dinner (often). Sometimes it was three of us and sometimes it was five. We went to the zoo, swam at a friend's pool, and walked the neighborhood looking for tigers. I rocked her to sleep, and she sang to me when she woke up. We read books, splashed in the bath, pretended to cut toy fruit, dressed "Baby," watched a tiny bit of Sesame Street, and played "Where's Mirabel?" under the pillows. She treated this house as her own. She knows where the animals (Beanie Babies) sleep, where the books are kept, and where her toys are put when we sing, "Clean up, clean up..." It was better than good ever gets.

Tears yesterday, naps today. And now we're back to life as we have known it for some long months. I don't mind too much. Marty and I are a good team—probably better when we don't have other forces, even loving forces, tugging at us. He's a remarkable man and we hold each other's hand. I like the calm time. It suits me more than I might have thought. I have no craving for the arts or the galas or the crowds, but I do miss the freedom of choice. A movie or a quiet evening. A dinner out or a barbecue in. A visit to New York or walking to La Jolla Shores pier. Options are freedom.

Day 188: September 18, 2020

We lost Supreme Court Justice Ruth Bader Ginsberg today. She was a rare champion and her sudden death, even at 87, compounds our apprehension and fear.

Day 191: September 21, 2020

Politics have been nearly all consuming and I have developed an addiction to news in all forms—television, print and social media of too many types. I will correct that bad habit soon but not just yet. We are forty-three days from the election and the stakes have climbed to a frightening height.

I've been working on a phone bank to Wisconsin, and the few connections I make with folks (most are hang-ups) have been fairly positive. These calls are asking them to support Biden. Later we'll make calls to help people get to the polls. The best of these conversations are with people who share my angst. Is our country about to make a massive change? Can we have a peaceful transfer of power? Can we have a peaceful continuation of power? Is it possible to retrieve decency and compromise? We don't know.

Over 200,000 people have died of COVID in the United States. 200,000! That number could have been, should have been, much lower. And yet, we may re-elect him. The Center for Disease Control, previously an impeccable source, has been discredited for politics, along with Homeland Security, the Post Office, and others. It feels Orwellian.

News today confirms that the virus is airborne and, at least inside, can travel farther than six feet which explains some of the contagion. San Diego has been open by our new measure of it. We've resumed outdoor dining and indoor capacity up to twenty-five percent, but that's all at risk now with a spike in illness. And yet, we may re-elect him. Schools are mostly closed. Learning is remote. Six-year-olds sit at their computers and follow the teacher's direction. Or try. Parents supervise and tutor. In theory. Trump's rallies are attended by thousands without a mask, at inside and outside venues. We are still fighting a desperate shortage of N-95 masks—the ones most needed for the medical community. Hundreds of vaccine trials continue but the president lies and says the vaccine will be ready in weeks. And yet, we may re-elect him.

My high school gang happy hour has been a constant. Friends of fifty years, every Monday night. It reminds us that the time is flying. I asked for a political check-in tonight and two answered, "No, thanks." That's how personal and threatening this time is. It may change our sense of unconditional love. Collateral damage.

The Padres have made the playoffs so maybe there is a God, but She needs to start paying more attention to the other stuff.

Day 196: September 26, 2020

In the last six months, few moments have felt normal and in those brief moments, something happens to jar us back to the oddness of this time. It's as if there's a gate around our lives and we walk up to it expecting to exit and then remember that we can't. We turn around and re-enter the life we've made for now. We know the virus better but not well enough, so it still defines our days. We cheat with a bit of visiting or entertaining or shopping, but we are always, always aware that we are cheating. We have drawn lines we don't cross — hugs, parties, travel plans — but honestly, we're all just guessing.

Worse, the virus has become a political demon with razor sharp lines, defined by resentment and resistance. One side thinks it's all folly. They gather, cheer, challenge. They are the Conservatives and believe the virus is largely a hoax. The other side, the Liberals—my side— sees this as an unending exercise perpetuated by those too foolish and selfish to make a sacrifice.

This time in America and in my life makes me heartsick. Pandemics and Politics. I'm anxious, sad, and worried about the world that my son and his family will live in. Can they make it right? They're up against so much. Mirabel is up against so much.

Tuesday night is the first Presidential debate between Joe Biden and Donald Trump. My wish for the night: May Joe Biden show himself to be a wise, thoughtful and caring man. May Donald Trump show himself. That would be enough.

Ann and Terry are coming over to watch with us. I'll fix a light dinner. We'll pretend everything is normal. Another election year. Like 1933 but without the German language.

Day 200: September 30, 2020

You can debate the merits of debate, but this was not a debate of merit. It was a carnival act, a shitshow, a spectacle, but even a generous high school speech teacher would not call it a debate.

Trump told the Proud Boys, a group of white supremacists, to "Stand back and stand by." Biden told Trump, after constant interruptions,

"Will you shut up, man?" Chris Wallace, the moderator, finally told them both, "Gentlemen! Gentlemen! Stop!"

The debate debacle had 73.1 million viewers—three times more than watched the Academy Awards this year but twelve million short of the Trump-Clinton debate four years ago. Viewers in 2016 didn't hear Trump refuse to commit to honoring the outcome of the election. This year they did. Seems this president is not a fan of the peaceful transfer of power. "There won't be a transfer—there will be a continuation, unless it's rigged."

God help us.

October 2020

"You Need to Calm Down."

~Taylor Swift

Day 203: October 3, 2020

The President has COVID.

Day 206: October 6, 2020

It's been a surreal week. First the unhinged debate. Now that we've had time to count, Trump interrupted 128 times—an embarrassing moment for America. That was Tuesday. Thursday night he tweeted that he had COVID. Friday he was at Walter Reed Hospital, and yesterday, with the grand gestures of Mussolini (one pundit dubbed him "Wussolini"), he returned to the White House, climbed stairs to the balcony, and pulled his mask off like he might have seen Zorro do. It was theatre—bad theatre with bad writing and worse casting. UnReality TV.

The bottom line: He'll survive.

In twenty-nine days, the polls will close. Election Day is now Election Days or Weeks. I have always loved going to the polls on Election Day, ballot in hand and, for many years, J.T. in tow. We would go into the booth, pull the curtain or, in later years, step up to the flimsy cardboard structure. I would lift him up and show him which dot to poke or lever to slide and we would exit with varying degrees of investment. Sometimes I cared just a little, sometimes a lot. Never this much.

I'm still making calls to Wisconsin. "Get out the vote" calls are easier than "How will you be voting?" calls. These calls are to like-minded folks who just need to be nudged to show up or turn in their ballot. Again, some hang-ups but, again, many pleasant conversations. Many of us seem to want the same thing and each day we want it more.

I just got a news notification on my phone that the Joint Chiefs of Staff are quarantining after the head of the Coast Guard tested positive.

He joins nineteen members of the White House inner circle who are infected.

Is there other life that goes with this time? There is. It just gets over-shadowed. Everything gets overshadowed.

Day 207: October 7, 2020

I am entering a contest at the library. Every year they challenge folks to write a story that will fit on the inside cover of a match book. This year *The Matchbook Story Contest* has been replaced by *The Mask Story Contest*. The complete story must fit, not in a matchbook but on a mask. That gave me an idea. I'm relying on a gimmick of two stories. One is read with the mask's pleats closed, the other with the pleats open. In the closed version, a horrid president wins a third term. In the open version, Taylor Swift becomes President. It is a time of puzzles and this one is mine.

Closed, the mask reads:

It. Was. Swift! Nobody thought a second term was possible, never mind a third.
We had spent 8 years believing that we couldn't be surprised anymore but here we were.
Post pandemic, crash, invasion, and succession. The President stepped up and shouted to the throng, "I'm not going anywhere!" A hush. Tears.
"What a crowd! This is the biggest crowd I've ever seen. Maybe it's the biggest crowd there's ever been in the history of crowds!"
Each person listening and watching shared one thought:
Everything has changed.
The President almost whispered, "You need to calm down."

Open, the mask reads:

It. Was. Swift! Nobody thought a second term was possible, never
mind a third.
We had spent 8 years believing that we couldn't be surprised anymore
but here we were.
Post pandemic, crash, invasion, and succession. The President stepped up
and the crowd exploded, "Taylor! Taylor! Taylor!" The familiar music
icon turned
global heroine, fearless against all odds, adjusted the microphone
and shouted to the throng, "I'm not going anywhere!" A hush. Tears.
And then jubilance more akin to a revival than an election night.
Taylor smiled.
She knew something about profound transitions, celebrations and
healing.
"What a crowd! This is the biggest crowd I've ever seen. Maybe it's the
biggest crowd there's ever been in the history of crowds!"
A knowing laugh rolled through the massive assembly. Taylor Swift's
smile was brilliant.
"The bully is gone. You belong with me and today we begin again.
Breathe."
Each person listening and watching shared one thought:
Everything has changed.
The President almost whispered, "You need to calm down."

Bonus points: titles of Taylor Swifts songs or albums—Fearless, You
Belong with Me, Begin Again, Breathe, Everything has Changed, You
Need to Calm Down

It won't win. I broke way too many rules, but I'm awfully pleased with my cleverness and talent with a glue stick. Version #1 has the menacing tone of today. Version #2 saves the world. I like Version #2. Taylor Swift for President!

Day 210: October 10, 2020

The second presidential debate has been cancelled because Trump refused to accept the virtual format. Seven states have reported record high hospitalizations.

I mailed my ballot.

Day 212: October 12, 2020

You can count the remaining days until the election on your fingers and toes now! I'm still making phone calls like each conversation will determine the election outcome, and I've had some lovely conversations with Wisconsin folks in the process.

One fellow today said, "I hope the first thing Biden does as President is issue an Executive Order barring Trump from Twitter!"

"I'm with you," I said, "but isn't that the kinda stuff we don't want our President to do anymore?" He laughed and said, "Maybe just one Executive Order?"

A young-ish woman named Amy Coney Barrett has been nominated as a Justice for the Supreme Court, replacing Ruth Bader Ginsberg. First, no one can replace RBG. Second, this woman wouldn't be in the running if someone could. She is short on experience and long on arch conservatism. Worse, her appointment would secure a super-majority on the Court just as decisions are being made about abortion and gun control.

Because we didn't have enough to fret about already.

Day 213: October 13, 2020

Yesterday was Richard's birthday. Tough times bring out the best in people and this tough time brought out Richard. A strapping young-ish Brit, Richard, a personal trainer, used to live nearby on Albatross

Street. Seven months ago, when COVID closed down his gym, Richard announced that he would be outside in the cul-de-sac on Tuesday, Thursday, and Sunday morning to offer a no-cost gentle workout under the Eucalyptus tree. EOA—Exercise on Albatross. Eventually we hung a basket on the tree, and we made thankful contributions but it's never enough to cover his gift to us—time to moan and groan and laugh and breathe. Under the Eucalyptus tree. Happy Birthday, lovely Richard. I wish every neighborhood had one of you.

Day 217: October 17, 2020

The U.S. has officially passed more than eight million cases of COVID. That's according to Johns Hopkins whose epidemiologist said, "We're headed in the wrong direction." Yup.

Day 218: October 18, 2020

My son, my best, my only, turned thirty-six today. He has always been defined with words like "zest for life" and "resourceful" and "sunny." This year has certainly asked the most of him, but he is bright and resourceful and kind—all qualities that will serve to buoy him if he falters. Kate and Mirabel are his North Stars.

I worry for his world, but this is a kid, a man, who will find a way if there is one.

Day 219: October 19, 2020

This week's cover of Time magazine is an illustration of a small White House overwhelmed with red Corona virus balls of every size. There are so many questions about the President's case of COVID. How sick was he and how much was forced bravado as he trudged up the White House steps, pulled his mask of and said, breathlessly, "Don't let it dominate your life."?

The world has now documented 1.1million deaths from COVID, approximately 223,000 of them in the United States. COVID has shut down businesses and schools, changed our way of living. But don't let it dominate your life.

Day 222: October 22, 2020 late evening

I have always cringed at the wishing-away of time. Whether it was a child wishing to be older or me on a Tuesday wishing for the weekend. It seemed a squandering of the most precious gift of all: time. But I am wishing away the next few weeks. For all the reasons of these last many pages but now for one more.

Marty seems to have COVID.

Day 223: October 23 2020

I'm worried sick.

I'll back up…

Last night we watched the second-should-have-been-the-third Biden-Trump debate with Ann and Terry. Cocktail hour on the patio. Moved inside and sat distantly with dinner from Kabob Shop. Separate serving utensils, dinner on a tray. We followed all the rules.

About an hour after they left, out of nowhere, Marty got chills and couldn't get warm. We layered blankets. His temp was 101. Oxygen (yes, I bought an oximeter) was 93. I gave him Tylenol and zinc. I fretted via text with a friend (everything remote), but there wasn't much more I could do except wait until he slept. I camped on the sofa listening without knowing for what.

Today, all his symptoms have eased. No fever. Normal oxygen. He's achy. Textbook COVID but mild, so far. A fair degree of denial going on here, mostly by him. He thinks it's a stomach bug—maybe food poisoning. To admit the worst is to surrender to the fear, and I suppose there's a chance of a different diagnosis. Either way, he's scheduled for a COVID test tomorrow morning. Day three of symptoms seems to be optimal, we are told. So today we wait.

We let Ann and Terry know. They responded like the good friends they are, "So sorry. Hope for the best. We'll cancel our plans. Let us know. It'll be whatever it's going to be." Unspoken: Oh shit.

At the risk of a jinx, I feel like I'm safe from this thing. Chase off evil spirits—poo poo, kinehora, touch wood. I just have a feeling with no very good reason. Still, I'm anxious and Marty's inability to be inherently thoughtful and factor in my risk right now is adding to my angst. Cough in the other direction, for God's sake! Wishing away this time!

Time. The default topic these days. Life after COVID. Life after recession and vaccine and isolation. Life when we stop framing our future with "after," and yet we are all experiencing a time that will be a profound part of us forever. We will never forget 2020. It will be our largest shared experience. Bigger than JFK and Dallas or the Moon Walk or 9/11. "Where were you when…" will be about a year, not a moment, but it will pack a punch. A trivia question on steroids.

Day 224: October 24, 2020

Three days. Six hours. Eight hours. Ten days. Back to that time thing again. Marty got a COVID test this morning—three days into symptoms. We should know in about six or eight hours. And in ten days the voting stops. If all of that doesn't make you anxious, you're an android.

The test was straightforward. I pulled the car into the dock at Scripps Hospital with Marty curled in the back seat. Petra came out in her space suit and swabbed his mouth. He gagged. That's that. Petra explained the notification process (phone call if it's positive, email if it's negative) and said, to me, "If he's positive, you're probably positive." It was a simple observation. Don't overthink it. So we wait. And wish away time.

I'm on the phone bank later today. Wisconsin is one of the critical swing states. It's gratifying to know that I've spent time on a part of the world that could have an impact but it's all still so gray when we are craving black and white. I will talk to folks today and pretend to be calm. I will say, "What can we do to help you get your vote counted?" when I just want to scream, "How is it possible that you haven't already voted for Joe Biden when the rest of the world knows that Trump is mentally unbalanced and dangerous AND MY HUSBAND MAY HAVE COVID!" And then I will say, "Thanks so much for taking my call and letting me hear your thoughts…"

I almost completely hate 2020.

Day 225: October 25, 2020

A cloud has lifted. The email arrived last night and read, "Your test results indicated that COVID-19 was not detected." Read: Negative for the Coronavirus. The lawyers had a hand in the verbiage, to be sure. "…not detected" has a bit of Cover-Your-Ass in it, but the message is one hundred percent relief.

As consistent as his symptoms seemed last Thursday, everything since has screamed stomach bug. It will pass. Literally. Thank God.

So now I resume my election obsession for nine more days. At least for us, for now, the load will be personally lighter. We have dodged the COVID bullet. Praying that the election arsenal is equally disarmed.

Day 227: October 27, 2020

Today for absolutely no good reason, on my walk I starting snapping pictures of the signs that tell you to keep your distance or wash your hands or wear a mask. Most of the distance labels aren't that interesting—just footprints on stickers every six feet leading into a store but some of them get pretty clever. "Keep your distance" is straightforward but add in police tape images or electric shock images or ask people to stay a dolphin apart and you've upped the game.

The hand wash and mask efforts are more clever. "No mask on your face, you big disgrace, spreading your germs all over the place," or "Wash your hands like you just cut up habañeros and you have to take out your contacts." My favorite is a local marque that, while urging mask wearing, says, "We can't control what's going on, but we can keep choosing kindness."

Day 231: October 31, 2020

Halloween 2020. Spooky for all the wrong reasons. No children ringing doorbells. No motion-sensor witches or tree-climbing skeletons. The candy won't need x-raying this year. An all-trick-no-treat Halloween. I don't mind for us, but there are only so many Halloweens in a kid's life and they all just lost one of them.

My precious Mirabel will be dressed as Madeline today, donning the costume for her mom's photo-shoot only. Blue dress, red ribbon, yellow cape, and a copy of Madeline written by Ludwig Bemelmans in 1939.

In an old house in Paris that was covered with vines
Lived twelve little girls in two straight lines
In two straight lines they broke their bread

And brushed their teeth and went to bed.
They left the house at half past nine
In two straight lines in rain or shine-
The smallest one was Madeline.

Except this little Madeline can't be with eleven other girls to break bread or brush her teeth and she won't be leaving 73 Harmon Street in Brooklyn. Halloween 2020.

The U.S. just broke a new record with nearly 100,000 new COVID cases in a twenty-four-hour period, which gets our total to nine million. Nine million. Nine.

November 2020

"Change is gonna come, oh yes it will."

~Sam Cooke

Day 232: November 1, 2020

I'm suspended between the comfort of possibilities and the anxiety of not knowing how this week will unfold. Anxiety is winning and yet, it's still a little like that moment before a diagnosis when you can pretend that it's still going to be alright. In two days we will know if Donald Trump will continue to destroy America; we will know if good won over evil; we will know if we are still the decent country that my father fought for in WWII. Or maybe we won't know for awhile. Right now it's the not knowing.

As of today, we're leading the world in COVID cases but the world is a mess. Belgium just locked down and England is likely to follow next week.

At our little Bread & Cie cafe, you can still buy a loaf of fresh gorgeous bread, but all the tables have been filled with frowning felt flowers and lovable stuffed monsters. For the rest of us, it's to-go orders only.

Day 234: November 3, 2020 Election Day 2020

Yesterday Donald Trump tweeted seventy-three times. Most of them were banal—"Good Morning! Let's MAGA!" Some were stupid—"We have more cases because we have more testing." Some were lies— "Joe Biden is promising to delay the vaccine and turn America into a prison state, locking you in your home while letting far-left rioters roam free."

A few days ago, Peter Baker wrote in The New York Times,

…with the election two days away, the consequences of four years of fabulism are coming into focus as President Trump argues that the vote itself is inherently 'rigged,' tearing at the credibility of the system. Should the contest go into extra innings through legal challenges after Tuesday,

it may leave a public with little faith in the outcome—and in its own democracy.

In things we can control…we met with architects today, on Zoom. We need to remodel our sweet house and put a master bedroom on the bottom floor. As screwed up as this world feels right now, I'd still like to stick around long enough to see how it all works out. We've got a better chance of that with a downstairs bedroom.

I guess that's today's version of optimism.

Day 235: November 4, 2020

We still don't know squat about the election results.

But there's that other thing…

Right now, 50,000 Americans are hospitalized with COVID and we're trending upward. In San Diego, we're screaming past the yellow, the orange, and the red tier and headed straight to purple.

Oh, dear God, not purple! As silly as this system sounds, the fact remains, the restrictive tier of purple isn't funny. It moves everything to outdoors again and dictates that gatherings must be limited to three households. What does households even mean? Is that like the fifties household with mom, dad, and 2.3 children? The Mormon/Catholic household of as many kids as God and nature allow? The household of our gay neighbors who are waiting to adopt? Seriously, who defines a household these days?

I think this election has made me cranky.

Day 238: November 7, 2020

Biden and Trump have both declared victory. Most media is comfortable calling it for Biden. Trump is screaming, "Rigged!" Biden is calling for patience. That sums it up.

Day 239: November 8, 2020

Joe Biden has been elected the forty-sixth President of the United States. The Associated Press, *The New York Times*, the "major networks" all say so. Pennsylvania locked it in for this fellow born in Scranton, and the final electoral count is 306 to 232. Clean as a whistle!

Except. Trump issued a statement: "The simple fact is this election is far from over. Joe Biden has not been certified as the winner of any states..." Nothing is easy with this man.

And yet, things already feel calmer. Joe did that for us. And it doesn't hurt that his wingman is a woman!

Biden. Harris. Onward.

Day 242: November 11, 2020

My grandmother would have been 121 today. Hazel, who we never called anything but Hazel, was a salty, hilarious, tougher-than-tacks pioneer woman. She was nearly a spinster when Fendoll, my grandfather, who we never called anything but Fendoll, rescued her from that fate. She was twenty-three. Fendoll was a catch. Hazel never really believed she deserved him. She was wrong.

Hazel was from family-who-got-here-with-Brigham-Young kind of Mormon stock but, as near as I know, never had much use for it, so when Fendoll proposed, his Southern Baptist roots mattered not one whit. Except for kowtowing to an overbearing and religiously fanatical mother-in-law, Hazel's religion met the end of the road on her wedding day.

I have a picture of Hazel that I revere. She is probably fourteen, standing by a very large heifer that is laden with three of Hazel's nine siblings. Her only brother stands behind the cow. She has taken a wide stance with her hands firmly on her hips, her long skirt irrelevant to her character. She's in charge. Even the massive heifer gets that.

Hazel was eighteen when the flu epidemic spread throughout the world. She turned nineteen the day the Armistice was signed ending World War I. She raised five children and buried two of them. She called her son-in-laws "jackasses" and her grandchildren "little farts." She did meticulous cross stitch, snuck cigarettes, read tabloids, and was the smartest woman any of us knew.

When I was a child and whined about something I wanted or wished, Hazel would mock me with the old poem, "If wishes were fishes, we'd all have a fry." That usually ended it. Later in my life, she was wishing for something, and I mimicked her old advice. She answered by finishing the poem that I never knew was incomplete: "If cow pies were biscuits, we'd eat 'til we die."

I would give anything to hear Hazel's thoughts about these times. She would have sharp opinions shared in lively language and I'm pretty sure she'd be on my team.

Day 245: November 14, 2020

The relief is there but it's 2020 so nothing is simple or sane. Two weeks after Biden's win by seven million votes (eighty-one million to seventy-four million), Trump continues to insist he won. No concession. No sharing of critical information. No respect. No normalcy. The victory is diluted by the knot in our collective stomachs—the old fear that a lunatic who convinced nearly a quarter of the entire country to support him is going to prevail.

Meantime, Joe has moved seamlessly and presidentially. It's a salve on a long-festered wound. He's not a perfect person but more and more I believe he is the right person for this complicated and troubled time. In a foot race where the health and well-being of our planet is the prize, I believe he will be the runner who will run fast and sure. He will know how to pass a baton and to whom.

On FaceTime tonight, our almost two-year-old Mirabel asked what Gra-pa (Marty) had on his shirt. He said he thought it was either dirt or ice cream. She replied "oh" as if that was the answer she expected. Maybe it was.

Day 247: November 16, 2020

We've moved into the Purple Tier.

Day 248: November 17, 2020

This moment in time can be hard on friendships. Our Monday night happy hour Zoom, with friends of fifty years, has been indefinitely suspended as of tonight.

We were so faithful for so many months and it was a sweet reprieve. Monday's at five, show up in your Zoom box with a cocktail and a smile. Easy banter from eight locations. But the tension was inevitable in a year that is so overwhelmed by division. The "no politics" rule isn't realistic when so much is on the line. How can you not talk about what matters? "Other than that, Mrs. Lincoln, how was the play?"

So, the break was made but it will come at a cost. Kay was my best friend in high school, my roommate in college, my friend and confident all the years since. Tonight, she hurled insults and I lobbed back. She truly doesn't understand why our differences can't be put aside and how I could risk our friendship on this mantel. So I wrote this letter:

~

Dear Kay,

I wish you knew how much I wish I could say, "We're going to get past politics and not do anything to jeopardize our long and precious friendship." I wish it was that simple but, for me, it is not.

It's not that we're on two sides of a policy. It's that we have a basic disagreement about what deeply matters. Kay, if you truly believe that a world run by Trump is better than a world run by someone else, you give tacit approval to decisions, behaviors, and policies that I abhor. You are willing to endorse a man who seems unable to tell the truth, even when it would support him; sows division with his citizens, the press, and the global community; speaks in hateful and bullying ways to anyone who opposes him; rejects science and believes he knows more than any expert anywhere; watches hours of partisan television and builds policy from those opinions; speaks hatefully about women and more hatefully about women of color; has an established history of business fraud and deceit; is painfully deferential to autocrats and tyrants; has enacted immigration laws that are lacking in substance, long on impulse, and fraught with cruelty; disregards and politicizes health policy that has cost thousands of lives.

I know you are fond of saying, "That's your opinion," but these aren't opinions, they are facts and if you want specifics on any single one, I will give them to you.

I am genuinely afraid of a world that is shaped by Trump. It is a world that openly and proudly hates differences, fuels resentments and, ultimately, I believe, turns America into a fallen democracy. I know you have an understandably sharp objection to any comparison with America now and pre-war Germany. Yes, it's hyperbole but the parallels are profound and undeniable. My Jewish son, living in the most liberal city in the world, is already experiencing some of the anti-semitism and hatred that Trump has unleashed.

In the simplest possible statement of it—I believe that if you support Trump, you reject me. If you accept his values, you reject mine and the ones I thought we shared. If I am wrong, give me the gift of showing me how I am wrong. If I am right, try to see your way to some understanding.

I know—it's complicated. I hope this might help you see how deeply personal and painful this is. I believe we both want a world driven by kindness, acceptance, integrity and fairness. Let's figure it out.

Pretty strong stuff, right?

Which is why I didn't send it.

It's a self-righteous, sanctimonious sermon and would fix nothing. It's not even the friendship I seek to save—it's my own energy. It's the power that I have given over to express something that won't be heard for an opinion I no longer value.

I've been so caught up in the rightness of my feelings that I'm wasting some precious energy and time. I can go on being mad about it or I can let go of the anger and refocus in a productive way.

I'm seventy years old, for God's sake. Time's a wastin'!

If a Zoom that demands awkward correctness is exhausting, get off the goddamn Zoom.

If a friendship is causing pain, give it a rest. It's not going anywhere. Take a seventy-year-old's version of a five-year-old's time out.

If another friendship restores me and allows a banter that makes me feel valued and wise and understood, do more of it.

I am smart enough to know the difference between toxic and nourishing, but sometimes I give myself over to the wrong one. Hazel would tell me that it's about figuring out what matters the most. It's about marking the jars correctly and knowing which ones to take from the shelf, which ones to store for the winter.

Reading a book, walking at the beach, seeing an image of someone I love on a screen, doing something that helps someone I care about— those are my life forces right now in this strange-time-to-be-seventy. That's where I will try to redirect even as I pay attention to my beloved, limping America and the course she is navigating. I can't change the pits in that road except in the small ways that make my life mean something.

No more screaming out the window. At least for now.

Day 249: November 18, 2020

We attended a shiva on Zoom today. It was for Andy, Marty's doctor and mine briefly—just long enough to diagnose my pregnancy and hand me off to his friend, Nate, for the delivery and my ongoing care. Andy was a fine physician and loved by so many.

It's strange to grieve on Zoom. The grieving is real, but all the ways that we comfort each other are missing. Still, the Jewish traditions do what they can to connect the process to a community, even if remote.

Traditions around death and dying are among the things I admire most about Judaism. Respect and caring for a person who has died is one of the greatest mitzvots (commandments, kindnesses) you can do. The 24-hour rush toward burial (at least compared to any pace I had known before) serves to hasten the soul's rest, but is also meant to allow those left behind to grieve, unencumbered by worries of death-related arrangements.

Shiva (seven in Hebrew) lasts seven days and includes services and gatherings, : (thirty) is the month of mourning, and *Yahrzeit* is for remembering on the anniversary each year. Those times are all marked with moments meant to honor the dead and comfort the living.

And always, the *mourner's kaddish*, a prayer praising God, and the expression of devotion that I love so much—*May their memory be a blessing.*

Day 251: November 20, 2020

Bizarro cartoon today showed an, old, bearded man, tired, beat-up and bruised with a cast on his arm, a crutch on the bar stool next to his and his cell phone at his ear. "Any chance the new kid could start a little early?"

Day 253: November 22, 2020

Sunday again. They seem to come faster than any other day. I still like them best, partly for the morning paper. I always think something will grab me. It doesn't happen often, but it still might. The book section is my favorite. Best Sellers is a list I could read anytime but Sunday morning seems like just the right time. I tend to linger on the obituaries and even say each name out loud. It's the least that I can do. So many names sound familiar. When I scan the dates, I'm surprised at the born-and-died years. They are less about my parents now and more about me. "Gails" are beginning to show up in the obits. Nearly all of us named Gail were born between 1946 and 1954. Makes me sad. So then I read the comics. At least a few. My dad's rule—gotta finish with the comics. It might just be "Bizarro" and "Doonesbury," but a rule is a rule.

I just wish we didn't have such daunting headlines. Like today:

- *At least five dead, forty injured when an SUV drives through holiday parade*
- *U.S. surpasses 12 million coronavirus cases ahead of Thanksgiving*
- *Trump tells G-20 leaders he looks forward to working with them 'for a long time'*
- But there's this one, too:
- *Politics, Science and the Remarkable Race for a Coronavirus Vaccine*

It's a fascinating story in The New York Times about the backstage efforts by Pfizer and Moderna, neck-and-neck to bring a vaccine to market.

Few corporate competitions have unfolded with so much at stake and such a complex backdrop. At play were not just commercial rivalries and scientific challenges but an ambitious plan to put the federal government in the middle of the effort and, most vexingly, the often toxic political atmosphere created by President Trump. Betting that a vaccine would secure his re-election, he waged both public and private campaigns to speed the process.

Just this once, the intersection of science and politics could be a good place.

Best moment of the day: a Sunday FaceTime with Mirabel. Today she asked, "Where's Gra-pa?" and when I produced him, she asked if he had on a clean shirt. She dazzles me.

Day 254: November 23, 2020

I had a colonoscopy and endoscopy today. Like Robin Williams said, "All orifices open. No waiting." Minor polyps, quickly resolved. The doctor rubbed my shoulders as I was nodding off. "You're very tense," she said. *No shit*, I thought.

Day 255: November 24, 2020

The young man I reported to in all my calls to Wisconsin voters dropped by today with a small gift—a wheel of "Jim's Cheese—Wisconsin's Finest Cheddar." He was effusive in his gratitude and praise. It made me wonder—what if our little band of Wisconsin dialers really *did* change the outcome of the election? Would it have been a different outcome if we hadn't each made those last five calls and convinced those last few people to find a way to the polls? It might be a story for Ray Bradbury or Rod Serling. What if we hadn't called at all?

But we did.

Day 256: November 25, 2020

Yesterday the Trump administration agreed to allow Biden and his folks to read the daily intelligence briefing and proceed, cautiously, with the transition. It may be as close as we'll get to a concession speech. That acquiescence, along with more good news about the vaccines, may be the reason that the Dow just broke the 30,000 barrier, in spite of hitting our worst day of COVID deaths—2,092 in one day—since last May. We are living in a curious time!

While all of that is happening, I'm reading to Mirabel on FaceTime. The book she likes best right now is *Moo, Baa, La, La, La!,* a fine work by Sandra Boynton with opportunities for flourish and dramatic interpretation. Each time, as I finish, Mirabel says dryly, "Again." It's not a question. So, of course, I read it again. And again. And once more. Can you ever get too much of a barnyard classic?

Day 257: November 26, 2020 Thanksgiving Day.

We Zoomed with our kids who are in New York and that was bittersweet. We Zoomed with our family, whose members are in Los Angeles, Portland, and Seattle, and that was joyless. We Zoomed with our other family whose members are in seven places not far from each other and that was tedious. Zoom never quite moves out of awkward. You could argue that it's a lot like how the real thing feels in person sometimes, but Zoom puts a physical and emotional exclamation mark on the sorriness of it. I am grateful for all of these people and the gifts they have brought to my life but I'll pass on the next turkey Zoom.

This morning's paper showed a cartoon of police busting into a dining room, guns drawn, with an accusation of "Eleven People!" (The rule now is a maximum of ten.) Perplexing times. I heard about a few friends with big plans to buck the system of a small crowd and instead of feeling like, "Hey, your choice," I thought, "You cheaters!"

Day 258: November 27, 2020

Retail sales online surged.

U.S. set a record for hospitalizations and patients in I.C.U.
Black Friday times two.

December 2020

"Nothing in life is to be feared;
it is only to be understood. Now is the time
to understand more, so that we may fear less."

~Marie Curie

Day 263: December 2, 2020

The front page of *the San Diego Union-Tribune* this morning is a cacophony in newsprint. "1,000 local lives lost to COVID" with pictures that make clear, each of these people was deeply loved. "COVID-19 Soars in City Jails." Ok, am I surprised? No. Do I need to care? Yes. Is there anything I can do about it? Hell, I can't even collect my neighbor's mail right now without scrubbing up afterward so, emphatically, no.

But then—"Panel Issues Priority List for Vaccine." Yep, it's the lifeboat story and I want in! The guidelines suggest that health care workers in positions of risk should be allowed the first shots. Then the populations within those places of greatest risk, like nursing homes. Ok, I'm grateful that I didn't make either of those lists even though I'd like to know when I will get the damn jab. It's all anybody can talk about!

Day 265: December 4, 2020

I decorated for Christmas today but I've got to admit, my heart wasn't in it. As Marty likes to say, "It's the least I could do and never let it be said that I didn't do the least I could do."

A scrawny short tree in the window and a few old faithful decorations—the stuffed elf woodsman, the obligatory poinsettias, the gold and red holly plate that my grandmother painted about eighty years ago and the sequined, tattered stockings that have weathered as many years as we have. They all found a place.

It would be a good year to string lights outside, but I'm just too lazy. What I did do was order dozens of teeny tiny Santa hats and stick them on the big dracaena aloe tree tips in the front yard. Those razor-sharp tips are suddenly less lethal, even happy, and so am I.

Sometimes a little is enough.

Day 268: December 7, 2020

It's Mirabel's second birthday.

Our precious toddler toddled down the stairs to see giant balloons in red, yellow, and blue and one of Elmo! Elmo, Elmo, Elmo! She marched like an animated toy soldier over to balloons and counted out, "Red bayoon, blue bayoon, yellow bayoon" and then she spotted the Elmo balloon and with her mother's help, grabbed it and added it to her bayoon bouquet. Her eyes were so bright, her dark curls so shiny as she marched around the dining room singing "Happy Birthday to Belle Belle!" Pure Joy!

I know all of this to be absolutely true because Mirabel's parents made a video and I have watched it over and over and over. Let me show it to you…

Day 269: December 8, 2020

There's a new "stay at home" order. It's hard to take it as seriously as we did last time but cases are spiking from our Thanksgiving gatherings, so the authorities have announced a three-week lockdown. Which means we mask up, meet on the patio, take a lot of walks. Modified rules for the rule followers.

A yard sign is showing up in our neighborhood—a declaration of faith:
"WE BELIEVE
Black Lives Matter
Love is Love
Feminism is for Everyone
No Human Being is Illegal
Science is Real
BE KIND TO ALL"
Sounds simple enough. Why is it so hard?

Day 274: December 13, 2020

Humongous, hopeful, happy day!

Cue the orchestra with the theme song from Indiana Jones or the first Superman. Turn it up. Louder! Go in for a tight shot on the trucks as they roll by: Massive FedEx trucks and USPS trucks and UPS trucks, one after another after another after another after another pulling out of a Pfizer manufacturing plant in Kalamazoo, Michigan, loaded with their cargo:

The Vaccine!

Three million doses are bound for over six hundred sites. If your hospital can prove they can keep it cold enough, they can have it. We've hit a milestone of 300,000 deaths in the U.S. but now we have hope.

Now we have hope.

It's been nine months since our neighbor, Dawn, explained what was coming and why "19" meant the virus was identified in 2019; nine months since children were told to stay home and watch the teacher on a screen; nine months since refrigerator trucks served as temporary morgues in Brooklyn; nine months since we clanged our pots and pans on the front porch at 8:00 pm to show our gratitude to the hospital workers.

Let the shots in the arms begin. They will start with those who are at greatest risk and then, finally, anyone who is wise enough to say, "Yes." Send me in, Coach!

One more thing—not nearly as big but big enough. Tomorrow is the vote of the Electoral College. In my long life, it has never been anything but a vanilla sundae for a policy wonk. I'm pretty sure that Mr. Arnold explained it to us in eighth grade civics class at First Avenue Junior High. I didn't care then, and I'd rather not care now but not caring now is not an option. In these strange times, as Trump still insists the election's not over, the vote of fifty states isn't simple. Inauguration Day can't come soon enough.

Day 275: December 14, 2020

It's the fifth night of Hanukah. I light the candles and say the blessing each night, but it's hardly been a festival of lights. Only the first night brought joy. That night, J.T. and Kate were ready for us on Zoom and while J.T. said the blessing and lit the candles, Mirabel sang "Happy Birthday to Mirabel" as she patted her chest. When you've just turned two and discovered the magic that goes with the birthday song, Hanukah must be confusing and, ok, stupid! It's a whole different tune and you don't get to blow out the candles? WTF!

Day 276: December 15, 2020

The Electoral College said, "Yup! Joe won!" Congress will count his votes on January sixth. Chief Justice will swear him in on January twentieth. We're almost there!

Day 278: December 17, 2020

My Christmas shopping was done, mostly, a week ago when I put packages in the mail to arrive in New York, Atlanta, San Francisco, Los Angeles. My gifts hit a different tone than past years. More reflective, I think. Reactions to the year we didn't expect when we unwrapped packages a year ago. Masks were not on anyone's list in 2019. Hand sanitizers in stockings, maybe, but they were fillers—not prized finds.

My time with Mirabel in August helped me guess at what she might like. I knew she would delight in an animated animal. Not sure how she'll respond to a chihuahua who sings "La Cucuracha" but I'm optimistic. The "whoosh" sequin pillow (yes, we made that sound when we brushed the sequins to display a second image) was a big hit on

Zoom in the summer so she'll open one with her image. Whoosh! The puzzle that spells her name may not matter on Christmas morning, but it will become something she likes, I hope. I'm only guessing about all of it.

God, I miss this time with her.

The vaccine is finding its folks and the increase in the disease lately is tempered by this ray of hope we're all feeling. It all got an unexpected boost this week when Pfizer announced that each vial can go a bit farther than they had expected. And Moderna is days away from rolling their vaccine out as well. The U.S. is still losing 3,000 people every day, so "soon and more" is the new mantra.

President-elect Joe Biden (gosh, that's fun to write) has nominated Pete Buttigieg for Transportation Secretary. Young Pete is about as articulate and intelligent as they come and he'll do a brilliant job. He'd be a likely heir-apparent if we weren't still a largely homophobic nation. We're moving in the right direction but that one has a ways to go. Our loss.

Day 280: December 19, 2020

I'm sitting on the patio on a glorious day. The world is still chaotic, but this place in this moment is calm and calm is a good thing. A squirrel just shimmied up the very tall palm and let loose a small cascade of seeds adding sight and sound to this beautiful afternoon. The sky is light blue, completely clear and there's a slight breeze that is mostly told by the bamboo. The birds are quiet today but we are urban here, so there is an occasional car or the sound of people working at home in their yard or with tools. It's what we do now.

It is six days until Christmas—a number that barely matters in this year. In a world awash in numbers, the ones that matter more are grim:

317 thousand: COVID deaths in the United States

1.85 million: COVID cases in California

22.5 thousand: COVID deaths in California
123 thousand: COVID cases in San Diego
556 thousand: Vaccines that have been administered
Almost zero: ICU beds available in the nearby hospitals
Skyrocketed: Companies out of business
Miles: Length of the car caravans picking up food donations
Two numbers that might give cheer:
Thirty-one days until Biden becomes President
Twelve days until 2021

Day 282: December 21, 2020

We keep hearing the phrase "…a time like no other" or the words "unprecedented" and "pivot." They were fresh a year ago. They are exhausted cliches now. We have run out of ways to describe what we have seen this year, from politics to pandemic, social unrest, family dynamics, economic hardship, physical and mental calamity. *The Washington Post* did a wonderful piece on the most used words of this year. The top three were "Exhausting," "Lost," and "Chaos." I have used them all, often.

"Lost." It's how I have felt and what I regret, especially with Mirabel. But lost goes further and the article, written by Eliza Goren, Shefali Kulkarni, and Kanyakrit Vongkiatkajorn included an apt summary: "We've lost our way as a country. The year was lost for students, families, weddings, holidays, positive human interaction. Lives were lost unnecessarily to disease. It feels like being lost in the wilderness with no compass." *Lost* is an obvious number one for all of us.

"Dumpster fire" was number six, "surreal" number five and "nightmare" number eleven.

A more optimistic take was the word "fallow." If I knew that word before, I had forgotten it but now I have found it again and it is one of my new favorites. Fallow. *The Washington Post* reader said, of fallow, "This is how I have tried to think of this year, a fallow year, a time of temporary stillness. It is easy to think of this year as endless, but it will not be. We'll plant again, we'll grow again. But this year, we just had to … stop."

A more positive, even calm, way to see it. I'm trying to think of it as a fallow year, this year of the great pause. But, mostly, I'm still with the kid that described the whole year as being a little like "looking both ways before crossing the street and then getting hit by a submarine." Yup, that's about how it felt.

Sometime soon, I'm going to start an entry with, "2020 sucked! Except for…" In fact, it will be a long piece. But not today.

Day 283: December 22, 2020

My walking, writing, laughing pal Marilyn gave me a wonderful Christmas gift—a writing class for tonight, the night of Winter Solstice. I'm grateful to mark the longest night of the year and this was a perfect way to celebrate it. We all settled into our Zoom boxes. The instructor lit a candle and our imaginations as she told tales of solstice traditions and then she turned us loose with a gentle nudge. Two hours zipped by with four write-and-shares. My first try was a scattered mess. My second was acceptable and a sweet memory was retrieved. My third piece, I liked. It was a venting that overtook me. The assignment was to write a fortune to yourself about the year that is coming up.

"You have eight minutes:"

I imagined the cookie snapping. I read the strip of paper's few words.

"You will have light."

That's it? That's all it says? You will have light? I don't get it.

And then Self spoke up and said, "Hey, what's to get? It's the Solstice! The calendar's version of a wake-up call. All that darkness stuff—be gone. Or at least be less.

"Your fortune, if you accept it, is a lighter spirit, a lighter outlook, a lighter time. Is COVID gone? Trump? Those 3,000 miles between you and your kids? No. Not just yet. But we're moving toward it. Moving toward the light."

Self kept talking. "You got very serious in the last year. Yeah, folks have been pretty locked up, or down, and nobody's having much fun. Sick. Dying. Pissed. Even those folks making the plexiglass dividers? They're making money but they're bored silly. And Trump? Oh dear! He couldn't be any crazier if he was headlining in Vegas with a trained chimpanzee, but he's still what you've got for a little longer. A little longer—not forever. The cameras will still follow him around for a while but you're approaching the DGS stage—don't give a shit. Biden's cool—with or without the shades—and a good man. That's the key. He won't be there forever—but long enough that things will be lighter.

"The damn virus is gonna lighten up, too. Kinda like polio or AIDS. Bad scar but history. So, be light! Light like an erased pencil mark. Light like Wite-out. Not even there. Except for that scar.

"All those relatives that don't care if you come to Thanksgiving next year. They're not gonna lighten up much. Never mind.

"Mostly, *you* are going to lighten up. Play more. Worry less. Laugh with your granddaughter. Yes, that granddaughter. Wear sneakers. Skip at the beach. It's time. And time is the greatest, lightest loveliest thing you've got.

"Let there be light."

I put the fortune in my coin purse.

Day 288: December 27, 2020

Christmas is done.

I'm always glad to see it end but never more than this year. Every year I dread the demands, but I comply and even enjoy moments through the season. Certainly, the last two in New York with the family were special times.

But it's always complicated for me. I'm not religious anymore. There was a time that I felt the Baby Jesus in my heart but now I live somewhere between skepticism and contempt, especially for the hypocrisy which, right now, is on overdrive.

And then there's the Jewish piece, which further complicates it for me. I respect Judaism and feel the most comfortable with it of any religion but even that leaves me wondering if it isn't all just man-made for us to find answers when there aren't any. A masterful public relations campaign to help us behave. This year it was Judaism that gave me many nights of up-close-and-personal joy with my darling Mirabel. I will forever have her image in the light of the menorah as she sang happy birthday to herself.

Today I was happy to get rid of all the folderol and jam all the baubles and beads and teeny-tiny hats and stockings and ornaments and candles into the two boxes where they live and lock them away, with a wish and a prayer, until 2021. Next year, I hope, a three-year-old will help me retrieve them!

The pandemic is still raging, and California is still locked down.

Trump is still screaming (in his ALL CAPS tweets) that he won by a lot and the vote will be overturned. Having a mentally ill president would be enough, but this year we have so much more. The next month will be precarious. We'll need more than a wish and a prayer.

It's interesting how, despite constant references to the contrary, we've all gotten pretty used to this pandemic stillness—this new normal. Marty's mom used to say, "You can get used to hanging if you hang long enough." A sad irony for her last bedridden years but she proved it true. Fact is, we are all getting used to hanging. When we leave the house, we grab our car keys, sunglasses and a mask. When we get back in the car, we take off the mask and use the hand sanitizer. We serve friends outside (and only outside). Blankets have become as natural for the end of the meal as dessert. We've adapted. Mostly.

Day 292: December 31, 2020

2020 is done.

It feels like we have exhausted all the descriptions and run out of ways to be surprised by this year. It was jaw-dropping, head-spinning, gut-wrenching. We are tired. We are spent. We are ready for 2021 with hopes that may set us up for disappointment but hope, nonetheless, feels good.

There is nothing magical about the line between tonight and tomorrow. There may be, please God, some magic on January fifth (Georgia's voting day) or January sixth (Congress accepts the Electoral college vote) or January twentieth when—please, please God—Biden is sworn in. But they are all imaginary lines of demarcation, necessary to our psyche but not official guarantees. Still, we celebrate the end of a year. Hasta La Vista, 2020. You sucked! You blew! You hurt!

My Christmas gift from my friend Barbara was an elegant, smooth leather binder engraved with "GVL 2020." I'm looking forward to putting these pages and some photos and other keepsakes in it as a time-capsule of sorts, but I'm realistic enough to know that 2020 has more miles to go as it blurs into 2021. We're not there yet. I used to say that some of the best '60s happened in the '70s. Praying that some of the worst 2020's don't happen in 2021. Too soon to tell.

Marty gets the vaccine next week. That is such terrific news for us, but the reason is a sign of the times. The hospital announced that, after 10,000 vaccines so far to all their front-line workers, they are desperate for "all hands on deck" so Scripps Health volunteers will be vaccinated and activated as they begin to vaccinate the general public. As a board member, that means Marty gets the shot, then Marty gets to work.

For the record, the U.S. is ending the year with these numbers: Twenty million confirmed cases, nearly 350,000 deaths, 125,000 hospitalized patients, and 23,000 in the nation's ICUs. Our own county's positivity rate is 13%, and San Diego has been identified as a location of the new, far more contagious, strain. Sharp Hospital nearby just brought in a massive refrigeration unit—a portable morgue. San Diego's first.

Marty and I will ring in the new year together, as we have forty-plus times in the past. I am more grateful for him every day. Tonight we will get takeout and look, again, for a movie on Netflix or AppleTV+ or HBO or twenty other options that offer everything and very little.

I bought a journal for 2021. There is something magical about a new journal. I chose "dotted" pages this year. Seemed like it would give me more options.

A final note on this New Year's Eve 2020. The official Pantone color for last year was "Classic Blue." Ironic, for sure, and not far off the mark. I'm encouraged that they have named the official colors of 2021 "Illuminating" (a vibrant yellow) and "Ultimate Gray" (a soft neutral). Pantone says it's the first neutral ever to be chosen. I say we could all use some neutral right now. Makes me wonder what other options were bandied about that board room. Something in the brown shades, perhaps, with crass undertones? Best to go neutral.

Happy New Year.

January 2021

"When our government is spoken of as
some menacing, threatening foreign entity,
it ignores the fact that, in our democracy, government is us."

~Barack Obama

Day 293: January 1, 2021

The San Diego Union-Tribune's political cartoon by Steven Breen is a baby with a "2021" sash wearing a hazmat suit and gas mask. Sigh.

Day 294: January 2, 2021

We have moved quietly and cautiously into a new year. Our New Year's Eve dinner was takeout from Bandar—Adas Polo and lamb kabob. A splurge for the holiday. It was hauntingly quiet downtown as we all dashed in and returned home. Our entertainment was a movie with Meryl Streep. The dinner was better than the year deserved; the movie, *It's Complicated*, consistent with 2020 but we snuggled up for it anyway. Marty went to bed at 8:45. He didn't make it to the ball drop where an empty New York Times Square felt eerier than downtown San Diego. (If a ball drops in the square and no one is there, is it still a new year?) I stuck around for a couple of the shows in the Twilight Zone marathon. It could've been a lot worse. It was, for many.

Our evening was meant to include Jon and Susan for dinner on the patio but recent cases in their building and new cries for "please stay home" made it an easy decision. Who would have thought such a nondescript evening could make a lasting memory, but good money says it won't be forgotten.

I got this note on New Year's Eve from Aunt Donna. She's eighty-eight now and I had shared some writings with her about the year and the political fractures our family has suffered. "A great write," she answered. "Sad, expressive, truthful, less demeaning than I would write and more blameless. I will never be able to forgive or forget those that made my life a lonely miserable year, ruined my income, kept me from relatives and friends who are no more, and even kept me from church in person. Just the struggle to stay a democracy. Who would have thought. One split nation under God. Poor Biden."

Time has been elusive this year but age is top-of-mind for those of us who aren't young— as if a robbery has been committed and even though we've identified the thief, the goods can't be retrieved.

Day 297: January 5, 2021

Marty got the vaccine! The first one of two, at least. An important step. He said the poke was a nothing and he's halfway home. <u>So</u> good.

The promise I made to cut off the politics after November third got the obvious extension (granted by me) when Trump didn't concede. Since then, it's been a long slog that, one day before the Senate counts the electoral votes, remains unresolved—at least in his demented mind and the minds of those who worship at his altar. There have been over fifty court challenges in six states. The president has tweeted every possible conspiracy and attacked officials of both political stripes. In a recorded conversation with Georgia's Secretary of State this week, Trump bullied and threatened and whined in ways that we all got to share when the tape was released. It seemed to matter not at all. Didn't make a dent. "How unethical," Republicans said, "that they released it!"

Ten Department of Defense Secretaries issued a statement full of admonishment with a whispered subtext to members of the military, "Stand down if he gets crazier!" An important step but again, of little impact if last night's crowd at a Trump Georgia rally is your measure. Do they truly (really, truly) believe that the election was stolen? Does Trump? Or is he just the most gifted grifter in our, or any, time?

So, they're voting today in Georgia. Long lines in the rain. You can tell the Ds from the Rs by who is wearing a mask.

Yesterday was a new single day record for COVID cases in California—74,000. Los Angeles has announced that paramedics can determine whether someone should be transported to the hospital. If they don't deem the patient survivable, they must leave them and take the next call. There simply isn't room. Or oxygen. Or staff. My heart aches for these young people who must make these calls, never mind the folks who are passed over and the people who love them.

We are in lockdown again which is still a vague direction even for those of us who have gone through it a time or two now. No in-person school, no hair salons, no gyms. Restaurants are closed except for takeout. No bars. All the charming outdoor spaces created by the restaurants sit empty. A few days ago, I waited outside a seafood restaurant for my order, and I was struck by the fresh lumber smell of their structure. So new and so closed.

Meantime, Marty and I stay hunkered down. Yesterday, I accomplished a massive closet purge. Today, Marty dropped it all off at the Salvation Army. I picked the bones clean on a chicken for curry salad while Marty broke down the cardboard for tomorrow's trash. Nothing remarkable for a retired couple. We make work and find projects. Tonight we'll have leftover spaghetti and watch Episode seven of *Bridgerton*—a period piece that provides a colorful, steamy fifty-minute escape. Simple pleasures.

Day 301: January 9, 2021

I'm just now ready to try to write about the last week. It has been a bizarre few days, and I'm not sure I know how to tell it but I want to try.

In the last three days, the United States Capitol Building was attacked, the Electoral College declared Joe Biden the next President, a Black man and a Jew have become Senators from Georgia, the sitting President has been asked to resign or will, in all likelihood, be impeached for a second time, and we have hit an all new high with cases and deaths from COVID-19.

The year is nine days old.

Back up...

Last Wednesday morning, I woke up early, desperately hoping that

Raphael Warnock and Jon Ossoff had squeaked by to win the Georgia Senate seats. The margins couldn't have been slimmer but what a magnificent victory! That would dominate the day's news, surely, but there would also be the Electoral Vote Confirmation which might be interesting since some sycophant Republicans were going to make a fuss. That's the day I expected. The day most of us expected. We did not expect chaos, violence, and death at our nation's capitol while millions and millions of us watched on live TV in real time and horrified disbelief.

We all knew that Trump was in a desperate state and was calling for a rally to "Stop the Steal." We knew he was making dead-man-walking calls to anyone who held a shred of hope for him. We knew that a few of the Republican Senators (Cruz, Hawley) were propping up his Big Lie along with many Congressional members. We knew that Trump was still using language like "Fake, Rigged, Deep State, and Fight." And yet, we didn't connect the dots.

We shouldn't have been surprised when his big rally, full of people he referred to privately that morning as "low class," included thousands who showed up to "Save America." "We will never concede," Trump told the riled-up mob. They heard what they wanted to hear and then, at his bidding and with the promise that he would be right there with them (which he was not), they began their walk up Pennsylvania Avenue. We sat in the living room watching a split screen—one with the time-honored vote on the Senate floor, one with a mass of waving flags and angry, screaming people. They reached The Hill, breached the barriers, and overwhelmed the Metro police. The double screen split into many screens to show rioters crawling up walls, heading down corridors, pounding on doors, crashing through windows, parading with bullhorns and stampeding through Statuary Hall.

Forty-one years ago, I was a young staffer on The Hill. I attended meetings in that Capitol building. I delivered messages to that House floor. My heels had clicked loudly through the echo chamber of Statuary Hall. Now, on the screen, I was watching a vile marauder with a Confederate flag in that sacred space, and I felt a personal violation.

It was terrifying. The rioters were from central casting for Mad Max. Many were bearded, slovenly, menacing in their red hats and military garb. An excitement drove their hysteria. Men were waving their cell phone cameras over their heads to capture the charging bodies, the wave of insurrection, the wild party they'd been promised. The ultimate home movie. They were playing out their video game fantasies—little boys in a feverish frenzy were the stars of their show and the world was watching.

Marty and I watched, stunned. We scanned the Internet, Facebook, Twitter, trying to get our heads around this. The mob moved into the House and Senate chambers and the mockery was in full view as these clowns—*these pigs*—sat in the Leader's seat, riffled through notebooks and took selfies. Debris from oxygen masks retrieved by lawmakers was joined by papers that were thrown and scattered as the looters celebrated their breach. It was otherworldly.

The rioters, who had erected a gallows outside, were now inside yelling, "Hang Mike Pence!" and "Where's Nancy?" They riffled through the House Speaker's office, stealing art and keepsakes—and her podium which they paraded through the halls.

Parliamentarian aides, evacuated with the legislators, had the foresight to capture the mahogany and leather electoral ballot boxes and secure them out of the chambers. And for the next many hours, people throughout the Capitol and into the office buildings, including the Cannon Building, my old address, hunkered down with fear and resolve. Good-bye calls were whispered into cell phones by congressional staff hiding under tables and in closets.

The mayor announced a 6:00 curfew. The National Guard finally showed up. Biden made an elegant statement in person; Trump recorded a statement on tape but it was fuel to the fire. Were we done? Maybe.

Senate Leader Mike McConnell, calling the day a "failed insurrection," and House Leader Nancy Pelosi announced that the vote would continue at 9:00 pm. At 4:00 in the morning, after one more objection by one remaining asshole in the Senate, the count was finished, and Joe Biden was confirmed as President-elect. A routine, antiquated ceremony was complete, and the country would never be the same.

For the next days we would sort and parcel the facts and the images. Janitors would clean glass and debris from the halls and Republicans would (mostly) denounce the president. Supporters for Trump would protest in cities across the country, including here in San Diego. Trump would announce, again, that the election was stolen and millions, including some people I love, would continue to believe him.

The inauguration is said to be moving forward. Trump tweeted that he will not attend. It would be his last tweet before Twitter suspended him indefinitely. About fucking time. Pence says he will be there. So will Clinton, Bush, and Obama.

There will, please God, be a peaceful transfer of power yet again.

Meantime, a Black man and a Jew walk into a bar in Georgia and the bartender says, "What can I get you, Senators?"

Baby steps.

Day 302: January 10, 2021

This morning, I posted this on FaceBook, with a few pictures:

This is my dad. He would have been ninety-nine today. He missed the last 34 birthdays but his legacy is enduring. He was something special — a Marine Corp officer, an educator, a miner, rancher, and finally, a veterinarian. And a great dad. He was tough, smart, funny and thoroughly decent.

One of the things he believed in most was critical thinking. Defend your ideas with facts and logic—and then bring it with passion. We had great debates around the dinner table, and he often took the other side just to challenge me—without contention or animus. His library included many books he didn't agree with but he believed in being informed.

In honor of his 99th, I'm going to channel my dad. I'm going to try harder to challenge my assumptions and work to gather the truth. I'm going to step away from those who seem to skip the critical thinking step, who are responding with passion but without facts. I can't change them and I just feel bad about the world. I'm going to invite meaningful debate but let's bring reliable information if we're to disagree. I'm going to figure out some way to make the world better. Ideas are welcome, especially if they involve U.S. Government and Civics.

Dad would like this. He would also tell me, "A bad man is leaving the White House. A good man is moving in. Now, pick your battles."

Doing my best. Happy Birthday, Dad.

Day 302: January 12, 2021

Mirabel has memorized most of the words to the songs in *Frozen* and she's nearly perfected *"Do You Want to Build a Snowman?"* Whenever her father goes into the downstairs bathroom, she knocks on the door and begins, "Dada? Do you want to build a snowman? Come on, let's go and play. I never see you anymore. Come out the door. It's like you've gone away."

Her father, behind a fairly sturdy door, just calls back with "What?" every so often. He can't know that his little girl, seated on the ground with her back leaning on the door, is just about the cutest thing that has ever walked the earth.

Day 306: January 15, 2021

Trump has been impeached for a second time. So what, right? One week after he incited insurrection, all Democrats and ten Republicans—only ten—have voted to impeach. Some of the Republicans said, "Yeah, he deserves it but there's only a week left in his presidency."

No, that's not a slippery slope at all.

Meantime, Johnson & Johnson has a COVID vaccine that seems nearly as effective as Pfizer's and Moderna's with just one shot. A good thing!

Day 309: January 17, 2021

Today is the last Sunday of the Trump presidency. As quickly as Sundays seem to arrive, this one sure took its sweet time. The chaos is quieting a bit. In the last week, Trump was impeached for a second time, DC has been closed to the general public, the National Guard has 25,000 troops in the Nation's Capital, and Joe Biden is, God willing, about to become President. That last point makes the other points bearable.

At home, we are struggling with worry and fear. Two days ago, my cousin had a massive heart attack on the eighteenth hole of his golf course. We're waiting to see if he will survive. The outlook is grim. He's my oldest cousin and I love him. For all the challenges of family, we would all be huddled right now if huddling was allowed. His wife can't hold his hand or sit by his side. It is an experience shared by so many—a devastating reminder of the aloneness of this pandemic.

If some sunshine can sneak in, this happened yesterday...

J.T. and Kate asked us to check out a San Diego house they saw on a listing. They seem to be serious about relocating to San Diego, and my mind instantly began to imagine soccer games and dance practice and the call to say, "Can you pick her up...?" or "Could you watch her for a few hours?" On FaceTime, I kept my repose. Stay calm. Don't scare them off! My feet, though, were doing a fast jig. Patience, Gail. But seriously, OMG!

Marty gets his second shot next week. I'm hoping for the notice soon. Another beam of light.

It's a gorgeous day in San Diego. I'm sitting on the patio watching the birds duke it out. They haven't figured out that there are two bird feeders—a kids' table and a grown-ups' table. They sing for me anyway. In three more days, Inauguration day, I'll join the chorus.

Day 311: January 19, 2021

Inauguration Eve. A ceremony in front of the Lincoln Memorial with four hundred lights lining the water of the Reflecting Pool. Joe and Jill, Kamala and Doug stand in collective grief with the nation as we mark 400,000 Americans who have died of COVID in these few short months. "Between sundown and dusk, let us shine the lights into the darkness and remember all who we lost," Biden said.

Tonight we will grieve. Tomorrow we will celebrate.

Tomorrow Joe Biden will become our President. I will wake early and plant myself in front of the television with the anticipation of a child awaiting Saturday morning cartoons. I will drink up warm coffee and grateful expectation. The hope of a new day. Another Presidential Inauguration.

Forty years ago tomorrow, exactly, I arrived at work on Capitol Hill two hours early. I wore a smart, gray knit fit-and-flare dress and brand-new gray pumps. I parked in the Cannon House Office Building underground lot and hauled my nine-volt battery black-and-white television up to the Congressional office where I worked.

Three weeks before I had joined the staff of the Honorable Clair Burgener (R) of California's 43rd Congressional. "Clair" to all of us (at his insistence and other Members' horror) had worked with Ronald Reagan in Sacramento and now, in his fifth term, was a member of the House leadership. A few years before, he had sat on the Judiciary Committee and had voted for Nixon's impeachment, even as a Republican.

In this last election, he had defeated Tom Metzger, Grand Dragon of the Ku Klux Klan from nearby Fallbrook—a brutal campaign that drew national attention. Thankfully, he received eighty six percent of the vote when the Democrats defected from their party to denounce Metzger and support Burgener. In spite of that fame and misfortune, Clair was a funny, kind, and decent man who was a respected legislator and beloved boss. His politics were reasonable, sensible and conservative. As his Press Secretary, I had no trouble representing his views or explaining his positions.

On the morning of January 20, 1981, Ronald Reagan would be sworn in as the fortieth President of the United States. Clair and his team were hosting the San Diego delegation along with two new Freshmen Congressmen and scads of VIPs from home.

I remember the moment when Clair arrived and spun into the office looking like Fred Astaire in top hat and tails. The Joint Congressional Committee on Inaugural Ceremonies had determined that proper attire in 1981 would be a "charcoal gray stroller jacket, a plain or pleated-front white shirt with studs, a dove gray vest, striped gray trousers, striped gray tie, black socks, and black oxford shoes." For women, dark gray suits were recommended—that was the entire directive. The dress code had become an item of some contention for its grandeur and forty-two dollar rental fee, given the economic challenges of the time. But the top hat prevailed, and Clair was going to own it.

Our office was decent sized as they go, but we were squeezed in tight. Folks kept coming. It was the rehearsal dinner to the wedding—which would happen just a stone's throw away in a few hours. Our team, just ten or eleven strong, greeted, served, schmoozed, refilled, and waved goodbye as VIPs headed off to file into the open space in front of the Capitol for standing attendance only. We cleaned up their mess and gossiped about their manners.

The mad morning was done. No meetings today, no letter writing, no lobbyists. We had a small TV and an open window with all the sounds of the inauguration. We were like pigs in slop. But then we wondered, *should we just cross the street and watch in person?* Four of us set out. There were no security concerns, no massive crowds, but our goal was still ambitious as we made a wide loop around the

Capitol and realized we had the best of all worlds back in Cannon 332, so we returned to our sound from the window and our image on a nine-inch battery-operated TV.

I still marvel at how little thought we gave to the freedom of that time. No metal detectors, no guards, not even a doorman. We came and went from the halls of Congress with a nod to protestors (there were always a few) but never a fear. What an unappreciated gift that was.

Back in the office, while watching and listening to history, my desk phone rang (that's all we had, of course) and it was Marty's News Director from WRC-TV. The station was short a couple of producers for coverage of the Inaugural Balls. He knew that I had some experience at that and still had Secret Service clearance from my time covering Vice-President Mondale in Las Vegas two years earlier. If I was willing, credentials were waiting for my pick-up at the Secret Service offices on H Street, four blocks from the White House and one block from the parade—which I would need to cross over. Driving or cabbing was out of the question so off I went in my new gray pumps. I ducked and dodged and, again, with little thought to security concerns, found the Secret Service office and found my way back, credentials in hand, fueled by adrenalin and awe.

I blew into the office and the staff waved me home, happy for a vicarious thrill. I bequeathed them my 9" black-and-white battery-operated TV and headed home for a quick change into the one evening dress that I owned. (I had spent $68 for it three years before and I still rocked it. Black spaghetti strap crepe, straight down with a large embroidered silver metallic flower on one side. Elegant and simple.) In fifteen minutes, I was in a cab headed to the station to meet Marty.

Gawd, he was gorgeous in a tuxedo! I have always told Marty that if we ever have a monster fight and I want to end the marriage but he doesn't, he should put on a tuxedo. We cabbed to the Kennedy Center and made our way to the media platform. From that point on, I was useless. I might as well have been a child in candy town for the lack of attention I gave my official task. Never mind. Marty had it covered. He would set the shot with the photographer, count himself down, scope the room for the interview—do it all without a hiccup. He even jockeyed us into a great position on the platform and told network reporter Connie Chung to move when she tried to stand in front of us. The man had looks and power!

Guests kept pouring into the ballroom. It was a garish '80s-style display of wealth with big dresses and big hair on the women, bigger hats on the men. Color and privilege all squeezed together. So many familiar faces from government and film—Reagan's signature and Nancy's passion. Bob Hope, Frank Sinatra, Jimmy Stewart. Hollywood royalty was there for their pal. Marty headed out to find an interview and returned giddy. In tow, he had Roy Rogers and Dale Evans. Seriously? In that whole menagerie of elegance, fame, and nobility, you choose Western stars Roy Rogers and Dale Evans in their bedazzled cowboy shirt and cowgirl gown? Seriously?

They couldn't have been sweeter. They were the perfect interview.

When the Reagans took the stage for their dance, not so many feet from us, my big takeaway from that rare moment, that moment that would be remembered always and forever was—I hate Nancy's dress. Single shoulder, white on white beads. I thought she looked old and boney with a tight updo and too much rouge. And then they were gone, off to six more balls, dances, and dress reviews (mostly glowing).

Ronald Reagan would be at his desk the next morning and so would I. A new era in government had begun.

Fashion Note: I walked miles and miles on January 20, 1981—all of them in heels and most of them in a brand new pair of Caress three-inch pumps. I went back to Lord and Taylor that week and bought the same shoe in cream, black, and navy.

Day 312: January 20, 2021

Joe Biden is President of the United States. I have witnessed nearly every inauguration of my adult life—two in person and the others from my living room. None has given me such an overwhelming sense of relief.

I woke late enough to miss the Trump exit, early enough to savor every morsel of Biden's beginning. I fretted as the clock in the corner of the screen counted down and quietly whispered, "two more hours, one more hour, twenty more minutes, two more minutes…" For weeks, that alternate ending hung in the shadows. So we watched the clock and, finally, the moment passed and a new clock started.

A time of hope.

Lady Gaga was grand! She owned—and wore—the red carpet. JLo was thrilling, especially when she cried out in Spanish "…con libertad y justicia para todos!"

Joe's speech was just right—straight talk from a statesman. Not the speech that will be studied for its eloquence but for its impact. Instead of speaking of "American carnage" as Trump had, he spoke of American unity and renewal.

America has been tested and we've come out stronger for it. We will repair our alliances and engage with the world once again, not to meet yesterday's challenges but today's and tomorrow's challenges. And we'll lead not merely by the example of our power, by the power of our example.

Kamala brought her exquisite smile to her oath, and every woman in the country knew something had just changed forever. Something good.

America's grandest ceremony—her installation of the highest leadership—was capped in the most elegant way: Amanda Gorman, a diminutive young woman in brilliant apparel and perfect ebony skin who brought the grace of ballet, passion of youth and blinding brightness of promise to her poem, "The Hill We Climb." Her lyrical verses ended with:

For there is always light,
if only we're brave enough to see it
If only we're brave enough to be it.

It felt as if the whole country exhaled in that moment. It was that kind of day. Intoxicating, satisfying, validating. Joe signed some executive orders without showing off his signature. Kamala swore in the three new senators (all Democrats) including one to replace her and then added, "Okay, that was kinda weird…". The Press Secretary did a briefing. The celebration, all remote, included music with trumpets, joy with exclamation marks, and masks — the ubiquitous necessary mask. A new kind of normal but, thank God, normal.

Normal. Normal, boring, ordinary never felt so welcome.

Joe Biden is President of the United States.

Day 313: January 21, 2021

Joe Biden is still President.

Yesterday, I got my first COVID vaccination.

Win-Win.

Day 314: January 22, 2021

My cousin is still in a coma, hanging on with his own sheer will and the help of science. Just. His wife and sons sent a note to all the family asking us to record a message for R.L. His wife, Linda, is being allowed in for a brief visit and will play them for him. The doctors aren't optimistic and it feels like we're all telling him good-bye. They've been married for fifty-one years, and I don't know how she will find the strength to leave the room when the time comes.

Cold comfort in the time of COVID.

Day 315: January 23, 2021

R.L. opened his eyes at 3:30 today. I think we get to keep him.

Day 317: January 25, 2021

This morning, I put on the same pants, sweater, socks, and shoes that I have put on for the last three days. Not because they are dirty or clean but because I can. Wardrobe has become irrelevant, and irrelevance begets convenience. Or laziness. Or both. It's not sloth: I draw the line at sloth. It's an indulgence that has filled the void of vanity. Vanity hates a void.

I just returned from the grocery store—one of my rare regular venues. I was thinking about how natural the unnatural has become and how, in this glowing florescent space, we have mastered the pandemic dance steps down the long, unevenly stocked aisles moving to *muzak* that never changed. Our baskets and masks are our shields. We check an aisle and detour if we see a few other shoppers. If we must pass someone, we do it wordlessly and with eyes averted.

Manners are a casualty of this time. There are many moments of thoughtfulness but the spoken words are forfeited for the proximity in which they'd be spoken, the air they'd exchange. No more "excuse me" as we step in front or "you go ahead" or "can you reach that for me?" The danger of breath.

At checkout, we stand on the mark on the floor—sometimes a picture or a pithy line about safety first, sometimes a bullseye (the irony)—until we're signaled forward and then we make a choice. If we want to buy bags (ten cents and more waste), they will bag the groceries. If we've brought bags, the bags must stay off the conveyor belt—which has been sprayed down—and we must do the bagging at Vons. At Trader Joe's, you have to bag your own stuff outside on a newly constructed worktable. At CVS, no bags brought in. They will bag it and hand it around the tall plexiglass shield. At Ralph's … and so it goes.

Nobody knows what the right thing is and they're all doing the best they can. At the heart of it is a monster germ and we're all playing keep-away without actually knowing the playground rules.

I miss eye contact. We don't have it on the street or in the market and, really, we don't even have it on Zoom with the randomly ordered boxes. On the patio, we're too far away; on a walk, we're facing forward. I thought we might, with face coverings, learn to smile with our eyes, but that requires eye contact. Today at the market, a baby, probably seven or eight months old, looked up and stole my heart. Direct eye contact. Behind my mask, I mouthed, "Hello, sweetheart," and she lit up like a sunrise. Babies see the soul.

Our housekeeper of twenty years just called. She has come much closer to mastering English, and she long ago excelled at loving-kindness. Maria was just checking in to find out when I might get "the shot" (we all call it "the shot" now). She's survived a couple of rounds of cancer in the last few years and at sixty-one, she's at risk for COVID, with many of her family members suffering now. Still, she can't find a vaccine. Between the digital and the economic divides, this epidemic has shown us another dark side of the income chasm. The haves and have-nots. She was so happy for me. I am so sad—and troubled—for her.

For all of that, or despite it, right now our lives are quiet, simple, even pleasant. We long for our kids and more freedom, but it's a quiet, painless longing, like you might feel on a cold day when you long for summer or the way you long for a special meal your mother used to make. A hazy-memory longing.

With the vaccine and election, there is renewed hope that life may resume one day soon. Our librarian, in a recent discussion on Zoom, said something that will be true for most of us and throughout the world: "When we are able to open, we will open to a new need—a community in recovery."

The world community in recovery. Are there twelve steps for that?

February 2021

"Do what you can, with what you have, where you are."

~Theodore Roosevelt

Day 324: February 1, 2021

In New York, our kids are snowed in. I'm not sure if it's easier knowing you shouldn't go outside or knowing you can't go outside but either way, these days, they're stuck.

Marty and I sent Mirabel a video and they sent back a video of Mirabel and J.T. watching it. I think we won in that bargain but it seemed to cheer all of us up a bit. We used puppets that have become phone call partners with us. Mirabel has named them Tomato—that's the girl, and Ging-ging is the boy (her ideas. . . don't ask me why). Marty and I—Tomato and Ging-ging—just chatted about what a cute little girl Mirabel is and how we missed her and it was all too silly for words. But, between her laughing at the puppets and J.T. laughing at his ridiculous parents, joy was had by all.

At the end of the video, Mirabel gently patted the phone and finally said, "Again."

Day 325: February 2, 2021

According to the Associated Press, January was the deadliest month yet for the pandemic in the United States. In January, 95,000 people died, bringing the country's total to 440,000. Still, the numbers are trending down, a direction expected after recovery from illnesses caused by the holiday gatherings.

Day 328: February 5, 2021

We are in the midst of a worldwide pandemic. Those words have never lost their power. The numbers are still staggering, and the vaccines are still slow, but things feel better. Between Joe, shots, daily press briefings, fewer tweets, and less news (my choice) in general, things are lighter, less dire. It feels like it might be okay one day soon.

That depends, of course, on the goddamn VARIANTS.

Variants. That's our latest dread and the newest addition to our *COVID Vocabulary List of Words and Phrases.* It means that this shitshow could have some additional and worse acts, different performers, more curtain calls. From the word *variation,* it's an innocuous-sounding word for a very nocuous possibility. Mutation probably is a better descriptor but honestly, that's a scary word and we're all sick of being scared.

A year ago, *variant* wouldn't have meant a thing to me. Same with *COVID, PPE, ICU capacity, Super Spreaders, Lockdown, Contact Tracing, Hydroxychloroquine, Herd Immunity, WFH, Essential Workers, Vaccine Tiers, WTF.*

Global Pandemic language. We're becoming fluent.

A year ago, being *positive* or *negative* held no threat. *Pulse oximeter* and *digital thermometer* weren't basic equipment.

I didn't have a *Zoom* account.

Hand sanitizer was a stocking stuffer.

Face masks were for skin care, left on for thirty minutes, and rinsed off with warm water.

New normal was a term that suggested a life change for someone else.

Pfizer v. Moderna was only of interest on the business channel.

A year ago, I had never heard of *Cancel Culture,* had never experienced *doom scrolling,* didn't know any *COVIDiots,* and hadn't grown weary of *"You're on mute."*

When we've put some distance between us and this strange time, we may choose to entirely abandon a few words that have come to feel like scraping teeth. Words like *unprecedented* and *extraordinary.* Phrases like:

"We're all in this together"

"You're not alone"

"These are trying times"

"We're in uncharted territory"

It hurts to think we probably aren't done with the word *Pandemic*. It used to invoke a B-movie plot that had a lot of men and maybe one woman racing in massive *PPE* and searching for . . . something. Now it's like finding out there really was something bad under the bed all along. It's hard to sleep well once you know that.

One more: *Fatality Rate*. Ironically, we've become immune to its malice. Our version of the Vietnam newsreels in the '60s. Armored against the charts with mountain spikes and casualty numbers, it only begins to matter when we hear a familiar name—as we all have now—ending with the words, ". . . has died of COVID."

New. Normal.

Day 330: February 7, 2021

Tonight the Tampa Bay Buccaneers pounded on the Kansas City Chiefs in the least-attended Super Bowl of the event's fifty-five-year history. There were 25,000 people sharing the stadium seats with 30,000 cut-outs. An estimated ninety million watched on TV.

Ann, Terry, Marty, and I were four of them.

Just one more memorable Super Bowl on a short list.

In 1967, my high school was chosen to send their band and drill team to the very first Super Bowl. I didn't get chosen for drill team, but my friends were there and sat on the sidelines before performing. I was proud of them, but it was a second disappointment for me.

In 1973, I hosted a Super Bowl party and won the pool of twenty-one dollars but felt awkward accepting it as the host, so I gave it to Sue who barely said thanks. It's still a bitter memory.

In 1995, San Diego was in the big game. We went to a party and watched Kathie Lee Gifford sing the National anthem, Tony Bennett and Patti LaBelle perform at halftime, and the Chargers get their butts kicked.

I didn't say they were great memories. Until…

In 1998, I served on the Host Committee for Super Bowl XXXII in San Diego—an unlikely task for someone who's not much of a fan. As the Sanctioning Committee Chair, my job was to review the applications of every group wishing to have an event associated with the Super Bowl. Official golf tournament, dog food, prayer breakfast—they all had to be approved and that approval had to include a commitment to the city who was their host. Our committee would verify each group's legitimacy; review their plans, venues, and financial goals; attach a community contribution, and then, finally, assign a member to attend each event and report back.

This position held unexpected power. The Ford Golf Tournament wants to give Children's Hospital five percent of their profits. *Okay, make it seven percent and you have a deal.* The NFL Prayer Breakfast will have gospel singers from Atlanta. *Okay, but we have some good choirs here. Include them and you've got a deal.* The Super Bowl Superfest is going to give us twenty tickets for city officials. *Okay, give us one hundred more so we can bring some low-income kids and you've got a deal.*

For somebody who doesn't give a rat's ass about football, it was a fun job. The big reward? I got the privilege of buying two tickets to the game. When Denver won a seat, I called my Broncos-loving uncle in Loveland, Colorado, and asked him to attend with my football-rabid fourteen-year-old son. It all made for an incredible memory for them and for me. J.T spent time with this precious man who could be my father's twin in looks and spirit. I felt like J.T. got a glimpse of the grandfather he didn't know and would have adored.

We made another memory tonight with Super Bowl LV, as we watched outside with two of our friends on a cheap TV connected to a long extension cord. None of us much cared if Kansas City or Tampa Bay won. Like many things now, it's about visiting old memories and making new ones however we can.

Day 334: February 11, 2021

I got the second vaccine!

The folks in charge of these shots are getting the hang of it. In a large parking lot cluttered with traffic cones and masked volunteers in traffic vests, I maneuvered into a lane and then to a parking space. A quick sit for my info, next chair for the poke, back in my car and over to the waiting area where volunteers put a timer on my car hood. When the fifteen minutes were up and I hadn't passed out or died, I was free to go home. Slick as a whistle.

I am fully vaccinated. The world is mine.

Day 335: February 12, 2021

According to the Lancet Commission on Public Policy and Health, approximately forty percent of COVID deaths could have been prevented if the U.S. average death rate had matched that of other industrialized nations. The Commission found that those numbers would have been far lower if the Trump administration hadn't failed to create and coordinate a national response. Instead, they left the planning to individual states. It was a cop-out that cost us dearly.

Biden just ordered 100 million doses of the vaccine from Pfizer, 100 million from Moderna. Dr. Fauci said that he expects it will be available for everyone by April.

Day 338: February 15, 2021

Susan and I walked to the pier on the beach today. We're both "double shot," but we're told to give the vaccine a few days for full effect. So we're wearing our masks with a small smile underneath.

Day 340: February 17, 2021

A new study out of Israel indicates that the Pfizer vaccine has resulted in a 94% drop in symptomatic COVID infections and a 92% decline in severe infection.

Many are concerned that this whole vaccine thing has been rushed. Doubters are gonna doubt. But even those of us who were comfortable believing the scientists about the science had a kernel of doubt—or at least some questions—about the full efficacy. This report from *The Wall Street Journal* is awfully reassuring.

Day 342: February 19, 2021

Rush Limbaugh has died. Boohoo.

That entry will be too strong for some and not strong enough for others but I believe Limbaugh was one of the first in the cesspool of radio and that the meanness he encouraged went a long way toward creating the hateful tone we have in politics today. "Even when I think I'm wrong I'm right. I am all-knowing," he said. Sadly, even as he mocked people and made vile sweeping generalizations, some folks believed he really was all-knowing. So, sorry. Boohoo.

Day 344: February 21, 2021

We're starting to hear the phrase, "A year ago today, I was …" more and more. We're marking the pre-COVID time from the COVID time. I suspect post-COVID will get here eventually. Forever a shared reference.

A year ago today, I was in New York playing with my grand-toddler. Mirabel's tricks included dragging stuff—a boot, a vest—around the kitchen island and looking at something with such intensity that you knew she was figuring it out—whatever "it" happened to be—a guitar, an appliance, a book, an expression. She was gathering the clay and playing with shapes. It was bewitching to watch.

Last night I did something I haven't done in this wayward year. I made a plane reservation. I've had two shots so tick-tock! I'm going to wear the latest travel fashion—a mask and shield and whatever else it takes—and board a plane to New York City. My two-year old grand-munchkin has all new tricks and I'm ready to see them up close.

Day 345: February 22, 2021

Today the death toll of COVID-19 in the United States passed 500,000 people. The President and Vice-President stood outside the White House amid hundreds of candles for a moment of silence, The National Cathedral Bell rang 500 times as countless families continue their journey of grief. It's been so long now, nearly a year, and many of us are a bit cavalier, especially since the vaccine has buoyed us with a promised end. But not so fast, sister—at least for many folks. Neither their healing nor their vaccine is in sight.

The pandemic story is largely about demographics. Think of a massive Venn diagram with all the colliding circles of age, race, culture, economics, education, politics, geography, physical condition. Every one of those factors has a million breakouts and every one of those make this experience different. Twenty-five-year-olds can assume that, if they don't bring this home to grandma, they're probably going to look back at it with minimal impact. Or maybe not, depending on employment trends and lifestyle impacts. Eighty-year-olds are thinking how lousy it is to have a precious year stolen away so near the finish line.

Marty and I are in the intersection of "white, older (not "old"—different part of the Venn), upper class, active, liberal, retired, urban, healthy." Almost every one of those are a rare gift, and this experience has been infinitely easier for us. Flip it to Hispanic, middle-aged, low-income, inactive, diabetic, inner-city, line worker, and this year has been hell. The spectrum is so wide and so complicated. We can never walk in each other's shoes, much as we might wish to understand.

I was struck on Sunday by an article in *The San Diego Union Tribune* describing how pages on the *GoFundMe* app often function as death announcements for low-income families. In "GoFundMe Pages Reveal Hidden Stories of Loss," Pam Kragen explains that the goal of fundraising on the app isn't so much the point. The page provides space for the thoughts and, yes, prayers, families and friends want to offer; to tell their father's or mother's or sister's stories and get out information they want to share—at no expense. A low-cost obituary page. Contributions may help defray funeral expenses, but the main goal is to spread the word of a loved one's passing.

The affluent, traditional alternative is a feature in the newspaper. *The Union-Tribune* obit, with a picture, starts at about four hundred fifty dollars and includes a link for those thoughts and prayers. All of this made me curious to look closer. The Sunday obituaries honored individuals as white as the paper they were printed on. Many of the write-ups included the phrase "surrounded by their loving family," which meant COVID wasn't the culprit.

Go-Fund-Me or the Sunday local section of the paper—they are all shared stories told about loss and grief with a hidden lesson on 2021 economics.

Day 350: February 27, 2021

The good news, bad news, hopeful news, terrible news …

Terrible: 510,000 deaths, 28.5 million cases, variants—most notably in New York and in California, are bigger and badder.

Hopeful: Six percent of the population has been vaccinated with two doses; a third vaccine has just been approved. Cases are declining.

Vaccinations are increasing. Congress is about to pass the COVID package of $1.9 trillion dollars, which will mark great relief for many and opportunities for fraud to some.

Bad: I've cancelled my visit to New York. I'm "safe," but my kids might not be, and it's possible I could take the virus to them. We need more information. My heart hurts.

Good: We're going to dinner on Friday with the "Anchor Team," the gang that Marty shared the news desk with through years of his TV career. We have all been friends for so long that we're old now—or at least old enough to be vaccinated.

What the hell do you wear when you're going out with friends? My memory fails. Just thinking about it makes my head spin. The good kind of spin. Like when you took a new car out for a spin or took a spin around the dance floor. We're starting to make plans again.

Finally.

March 2021

"Time is the longest distance between two places."

~Tennessee Williams

Day 352: March 1, 2021

The Golden Globes were on TV tonight and COVID was, again, the featured performer. The virtual ceremony honored shows that had seen us through a virtual year. It was awkward and generally unsatisfying. But the winners, long in production before this year's fate was known, somehow spoke to our lives.

The Queen's Gambit, Schitt's Creek, and *The Crown* were our escapes when we needed them most. As Moira would say, "I'd kill for a good coma right now."

Nomadland took best picture. It's a movie about loss and journey, poverty, kinship, loneliness, and hard work. It was a sad, spare movie in this sad, spare time. The director, 38-year-old Chloe Zhao, accepted from her computer in an unadorned office and toasted us with her coffee mug.

Finally, Jane Fonda, who inspires awe in some and contempt in others, was presented with the Cecil B. DeMille Award and made a stirring speech about inclusion. "In turbulent, crisis-torn times like these, storytelling has always been essential. You see, stories have a way that can change our hearts and our minds and help us see each other in a new light—to have empathy and to recognize that for all of our diversity, we are all humans first."

If the stories we are telling in 2021 can't move us toward that, nothing can.

Day 360: March 9, 2021

This space of time between this March and our last one will fill libraries when its history is written. In 2020, the traditional reference for perfect vision, we've had a look at much that is imperfect. Nature, science, humankind. We have gone through a time of hope and desperation. A cautionary tale to be sure. We have seen that when people go inside, nature flourishes. When kindling is lit, infernos result. When science leads, prevention follows. When racism is allowed, decency can be overwhelmed.

Next Monday is the one-year anniversary of the lockdown and we are all changed for it in large and small ways. I have learned that I like quiet and inactivity more than I knew. I believe, more than ever, that I was lucky to marry the man I did. His decency and gentleness have kept us balanced. I can cook things I never tried before, and I can go weeks without driving anywhere. I have learned that relationships that seemed unbendable can, in fact, snap like a twig. I've learned that some relationships are now, for experiences of this year, part of my soul.

I no longer believe that time heals all wounds. I believe some wounds are so deep that time can sometimes even fester them. I have developed a dueling sense of fear and hope for my children's future, but I know it is almost entirely up to them and I regret that my generation didn't do better in our bequest.

I believe that one of our realized tragedies of this time is that families live so far from each other. That fact added immeasurably to the heartache of 2020 for rich and poor alike.

I've rebooked my New York trip. If my kids can be safe around me, it's time. I need to wrap my arms around all of them. In 2021, I'm reminded that nothing will ever matter more.

Day 361: March 10, 2021

Cracks in the wall slowly let light through.

After a CDC adjustment allowing those who are vaccinated to gather without masks, we have joined friends for dinner three times in one week. All outside and chilly but still, celebrations with laughter and conversation. Friends together on perfect San Diego nights.

On Sunday I drove to Orange County to take Aunt Donna to lunch for her birthday. We sat on a sweet patio and celebrated the beginning of her ninetieth year.

The U.S. is averaging two million shots a day. One in ten adults has been vaccinated. Big, big numbers that allow the little things—like time with people we love.

Day 362: March 11, 2021

I've been thinking a lot about bravery lately.

I believe it was profoundly brave of Joe Biden to run for president. Maybe not in his past campaigns but in this one. He's too old and he must know that. His physical safety is at risk for all the craziness of the time. His strength and overall stamina are not optimum for any tough job, never mind the toughest. I don't believe it was about ego for this imperfect man. It was because he understood that he had a rare combination of skill and experience to actually save a failing nation. I will always believe that his service now is an act of extraordinary courage for all the right reasons.

That kind of bravery is in a separate category. Mostly, I've been thinking about the bravery of everyone who has had an active, physical part in this crisis. We've gotten used to the phrase "front-line workers," and they are mostly people who have otherwise never known the front line or certainly the front row. The health care workers, caregivers, clerks and waiters, drivers and cleaners. Their courage may be rooted in their need for an income, but it doesn't change how much we've needed their help and how hard it must be for them just to show up every day.

Getting the shot requires a certain bravery. A sharp instrument plunged into our skin injecting foreign chemicals into our bodies. For those afraid of needles or a bit skeptical, it is a brave step. I think it's braver, as some are still doing, to wait their turn.

Mostly, I see the bravery of those who face the greatest loss and fear of this time. When my cousin R.L.'s survival seemed lost, his wife, unable to speak to him or hold his hand, was the face of bravery. For those with their hands against the window as a failing loved one nods back—that's the face of bravery. For those who show up the next day and screw up the courage to ease the pain or share the weight or keep the promise, that's the face of bravery. That's also the face of hope and goodness. I hope we prove worthy of it.

Day 365: March 14, 2021

"We are getting back to normal." That's the catchphrase of late, rarely said with true conviction.

We remember normal and we're sure not there yet, but with shots and motivation, we're ready to give it a go. Our re-entry friends are the same ones that we exited with last March. Can we really pick up where we left off? Let's try.

We've had three gatherings this week—all inside without masks. We've talked a lot about the awkwardness in this newfound (or rediscovered) familiarity. We all feel as if we are doing something wrong. Very wrong.

But it feels very good.

Last night, Bill and Natalie and Adam and Todd came for dinner. The young'uns, Todd and Adam, haven't been vaccinated yet so we ate our chili outside with blankets nearby. Todd, who's been San Diego's mayor for three months, said he has a staff of thirty people, many of whom he has never met in person. Natalie, a former FBI agent and life-long "tough broad," is on this side of her second round of chemo. She is fragile and tentative. Bill, San Diego's sheriff, is always bright and positive even as the weight of the world, including his wife's illness and COVID in the jails, is on his shoulders.

We still managed a brief sense of respite from all that is hard right now.

Today, Janine and Sandy along with Arlene came for lunch. We're all vaccinated so we sat in the dining room. I'd forgotten how lovely and calm that space is, and the conversation was as warm as the air.

Janine, a retired anesthesiologist, has been vaccinating people at clinics all over San Diego. She said that, of the 2,412 shots she's administered so far (she's keeping track by noting the number of Band-Aid boxes she goes through), only one fellow was truly contrite. She asked him the obligatory pre-shot questions and was met with muffled answers and harrumphs. When she got to the last one and asked, "Do you give me permission to give you this vaccine?" he answered, "If I want to stay married, I'd better say yes."

Arlene, a Rabbi, talked about her tasks—nearly all remote. She had spent the morning helping with a virtual funeral in Los Angeles, had virtually counseled a couple about their upcoming marriage and said, casually, "Right now I'm at a virtual conference but we've adjourned for lunch." There are some advantages to Zoom. You can, kind of, be two places at once. When Arlene arrived at our house, I greeted her with a hug—CDC says we can—and she shed a few tears. It's a lonely time, no matter how busy you might be.

Finally, we had a sweet evening on Friday with Marilyn and her sort-of-beau, Bob. He's a lovely man who brings so many gifts to our friendship and to their courtship, but in some curious ways, I know that COVID has been a convenient barrier to any emotional or intimate commitment between them. It made me think, again, about what a challenging time it is for relationships of any age or ilk. Right now, couples who have weathered enough to know that they will weather this might be the exception, but the year has asked hard questions of couples, revealing us as individuals and as partners. The results may lead to stronger pairings and deeper commitments or more contentious splits. Perhaps Post-COVID will bring a glut of births and divorces.

Day 366: March 15, 2021

Big week ahead for me. First, I get a tooth. Front and center tooth. Hee-haw tooth. I broke it off six weeks ago today (damn Super Bowl pizza) and, but for the mandatory masks, would have spent $1200 for a temporary replacement. I've weathered a few awkward moments and have learned the closed mouth smile reminiscent of retainer days but tomorrow, God willing, I'll have a full set again. Then on Tuesday, I get my gray gone.

With all that repaired protein, I'm off on Wednesday to New York to see my precious Mirabel and her remarkable parents. There will be hugs!

Kate got her vaccine today, qualified by her asthma. J.T. has an appointment in the morning—a hand-me-down from a friend. I'm thrilled for their opportunity, their assertiveness, and, yes, their privilege. Even in moments of gratitude, we must recognize that for what it is: another example of "have and have-not." Still, it's a hopeful sign. More young people getting the jab. Post-COVID in sight.

Maybe that damn tunnel's got light in it after all. Headlamps in place—dawn ahead. "Second star to the right and straight on 'til morning."

Day 368: March 17, 2021

I'm on an airplane headed to New York City! It's been exactly six months since I hugged my granddaughter, and I'm five and half months past due. I will bask in every moment of the next four days!

But first I have to get there.

The airline industry has changed to meet this post-worst-of-COVID moment. The cavernous terminal has a light crowd, and we are greeted with stanchions telling us to line up and floor markers telling us where to stand. I stop on a surfboard image six feet from the wave image six feet from the toes-in-the-water image, headed to security clearance. The floor tags are showing wear, some frayed edges that say that others have stood there, too. I find comfort in that.

At the TSA desk, more silence. The old banter, however forced it was, is no longer necessary. I hand the agent my ID, he glances up to my face, signals to drop my mask, looks at my eyes, and waves me along. We don't speak.

Beyond security, passengers continue their quiet passage. The sound of luggage wheels is interrupted as a mother calls out to her child who has, like a child, made a dash down the corridor. This muffled reprimand, with its familiar sound, brings a hint of normalcy. At the gate, empty seats are marked with a crossed-out circle announcing, "For your safety." The unmarked seats show depressions and proof of compliance.

We are all venturing forward as if the ice may break and we'll fall in.

I had just settled when a nearby exchange broke out.

"This is such bullshit," he said to his wife but, really, to all of us in earshot.

"We talked about this, and you promised you would not make a fuss."

"I'm not making a fuss. I'm just saying that this is bullshit." He tugged at his mask.

His wife looks like me. She's almost certainly an anxious grandparent newly vaccinated, and this scene is obviously what she had feared. As travel has begun to increase, so have the stories about angry passengers wanting freedom their own way.

"Please!" she said in a whisper.

"I'm just saying it's bullshit. I'm going to go get a doughnut. They can't arrest me for not wearing a mask if I'm eating a doughnut."

He lumbered toward the only line at the airport—the stand where coffee and doughnuts are in demand. His wife, sitting alone, bears a tension that we all understand.

Onboard, the plane feels like a refuge. So here I sit in a row by myself, tucked in by the window, double masked and, occasionally, shielded. The flight attendant has checked his manifest and, fully masked, just welcomed me back, noting that it's been a year. Even his whispered welcome through the mask jars me.

He hands me a small unimprinted baggie with an eight-ounce water bottle (hydration), a tiny bag of almonds (protein), a package of two

Delta biscotti (sweet), a Purell wipe (safety), and a note advising us of free Wi-Fi (compensation). Seems a worthy alternative to last year's meager box-lunch of cheese and crackers. We are all—or almost all—learning to be grateful for the small things, finding a new understanding of what is enough.

I'm grateful that the doughnut man is many rows back. I'm grateful that I've been vaccinated. I'm grateful for the beautiful child that I'm soon to see.

My carry-on is weighted with a little rabbit family and their kitchen along with a magnetic veterinary hospital and some notes from Tomato and Ging-ging, the puppets we have played with on Zoom. All for Mirabel. I'll travel lighter—in some ways—when I return home.

Day 373: March 22, 2021

New York was perfect. Four days of bliss that anchored me, made me laugh and, finally, made me cry. Truly, there is no way to fairly describe the way it feels to be loved by a child who is of your own child. We took walks, played with the bunny family, discovered an "adorable invisible mouse" who toots. (Toots a lot, actually, and it's always funny. What is it about bathroom humor?) We pretended we were on a boat, in a plane, and on a horse.

We read many, many books (*There's a Bear in my Chair, Llama Llama Red Pajama*) and sang many songs ("Baby Shark," and "Five Little Monkeys," and "I'm a Little Teapot"). She sang "Let it Go" and finished each time with the spoken words, "The cold never bothered me anyway," her arms crossed and on her face, a serious scowl.

I was there for her first Shirley Temple mocktail and her reaction, "Oh My Goodness!" and then we froze as we sat outside eating burgers and fries. They have never tasted better.

We found three playgrounds and on the last day, when her parents had been missing just a few moments too long (they'd escaped for a rare Sunday brunch and time alone) and all the other moms and grandmas except me had come prepared with a snack, she announced, with a wagging finger, "I think it's time for you to go home." But then, later, she hugged me for a very long time when I did.

In a normal world, she would know me so much better. We would have visited at least every few months. But this world isn't ready to be normal yet, so I don't know when I will see her again. Her parents are vaccinated. Her grandparents are vaccinated. But she is still at risk. Just a little, but that is far too much.

My final melancholy moment came with the ride to the airport. It's the first time I've been driven by a stranger in over a year. My Uber driver was a lovely man, quick with the luggage and early morning greeting. His English was adequate, but our entire conversation took place in the first few moments. He asked if I was on vacation. I said no, just visiting family. He said family is everything. I nodded. And then he drove and I sat and we exchanged nothing else, knowing that masks and COVID made it an unnecessary luxury. I know that in another time we would have had a sweet exchange. I would have heard about his children, his borough, the hours he's working now. He would have heard about Mirabel and her songs and how much I will miss her. He delivered me safely, our eyes met with their smiles, and we went to our separate lives.

Day 379: March 28, 2021

A year ago I wrote that this wasn't fun anymore. It still isn't.

San Diego's in Red Tier. Hopes faded for Orange this morning and we will wait another week. California's Department of Public Health created the tier system to define the level of danger based on number of cases and the percentage of positive COVID tests. And to scare the hell out of us.

Per CDPH:

The purple (Widespread) tier threshold will remain at greater than 10 cases per 100,000, Red (Substantial) tier case rate range will narrow to 6–10 cases per 100,000; and the Orange (Moderate) tier case rate range will shift to 2–5.9 cases per 100,0000.

Blah blah blah. Numbers and more numbers. In application terms, the Red tier means a lot of businesses have to close again, some can open but only at 25% capacity and I can't go back to get my hair done.

Meantime, COVID is spiking in many parts of the country and the CDC Director teared up on television this week, saying that she has a sense of "impending doom." A fourth wave is possible, even probable. Those of us with the vaccine seem to be safe. San Diego seems to have stabilized. That is the update. That's it. Stand by.

Day 382: March 31, 2021

We've managed our second Seder on Zoom. My table was perfect again with our Jewish heirloom candlesticks, my mom's fine crystal and flowers from the garden. Marty's sister, Jan, came down which was a surprise and a treat. She's been very isolated so this was a big step. Down and back to Los Angeles but a start for her and a nice reconnection for us.

Passover is all about seeking freedom. A familiar and timely theme. Check the comparisons . . . 382 days in masks vs. forty years stuck in the desert. COVID symptoms vs. boils and toads and storms and darkness and six more including death of the firstborn. Shortage of yeast starter vs. unleavened bread. Chilling rule by the GOP vs. cruel rule by Egyptians. Okay, maybe we compete with that one. Hard to know. Time and Place.

Our pandemic vernacular is beginning to be replaced with words and phrases like "looking ahead" or "returning to." Sunday's paper included a business column with reasons we can be optimistic in San Diego. The list included resurgence of the hospitality industry, acceleration in technology innovation (especially in our biotech industry), the speed of the vaccine and, of course, a pent-up need for fun, travel and entertainment. Today at Home Depot I waited in a long line to buy a can of paint. At the register, through all the plexiglass and my mask, I asked the cashier if it was always this crazy on a Wednesday and he said, "The stimulus checks have arrived." Shoppers had carts filled with basics but also a plant or a potted flower or a pillow for the patio. Even in the tough times, we're seeking some beauty and joy.

Meantime, I'm shaking off the blues. J.T. and Kate made an offer, a good one, on another home and, again, got outbid. I had allowed myself to imagine them in that house. I had even imagined myself there. On the patio or helping in the kitchen or playing in the yard with my Mirabel.

Not yet.

Patience, Mimi.

Our Wisteria is in full bloom. Paler than last year—we all are—but exquisite. The bougainvillea is busting out and the roses are ready to share. The orange tree has that magical fragrance of the blossom and some of the fruit is begging to be juice. Our little lemon and lime trees are limping along but still determined to add to our basket. The figs are daring a critter to take them. One will. San Diego is glorious, warm, fragrant, clear. The birds think we don't notice their construction. It's such a sweet game of hide and seek. Hope in the air.

It's spring.

April 2021

"Life is a shipwreck, but we must not forget to sing in the lifeboats."

~Voltaire

Day 384: April 2, 2021

San Diego Union-Tribune front page:
- *Padres Open the Season with 8,873 Fans in the Stands*
  - *UCSD to immunize 12,000 students*
  - *30% of State has Received One Dose of Vaccine*
  - *Eligibility Expands to Age Fifty and Up This Week*
  - *Roller Coasters at Belmont Park and LegoLand are Rolling*

There seems to be a corner. We seem to be turning it.

Day 387: April 5, 2021

In this Pandemic Record, as I've come to think of it, the edges of the last nearly four hundred days have bled beyond COVID into politics, government, family, friendships, and all the things that have been part of this upside-down year. So many books will be written about 2020 and perhaps much of 2021. My wish for this personal account is that it can add to the conversations we will have in the years ahead. Discussing how many angels can sit on the head of a pin now seems like an ordinary debate.

Case in point—QAnon. I've talked about them before. If there is a symbol for all the parts of this time that are truly messed up, it might be the desperate and damaging conspiracy theory known as QAnon. I don't believe I know any members of this group, but anyone who knows my values wouldn't admit their membership to me. To be part of "The Q" is to believe the preposterous.

From Wikipedia:

QAnon[a] (/ˌkjuːəˈnɒn/), or simply Q, is a disproven and discredited American far-right conspiracy theory alleging that a secret cabal of Satan-worshipping, cannibalistic pedophiles was running a global child sex-trafficking ring and plotted against former U.S. president Donald Trump while he was in office. QAnon is commonly called a cult.

A cult? Thank you, Captain Obvious. QAnon is a craziness with elements of racism, anti-Semitism, desperation, illiteracy, and ignorance. It is an extreme example, to be sure, but it speaks to these times and how we have split apart in ways that don't make sense. It's hard to imagine a path forward when so many are willing to believe the unbelievable.

It is our nature to be fascinated by conspiracy. As a college girl, I huddled with others around the turntable as we studied the lyrics that proved that Beatle Paul was dead. All the evidence was right in front of our ears. Tragic but undeniable.

Some believe that JFK was assassinated by Russians, Barack Obama wasn't born in the U.S., contrails from airplanes are chemical weapons, and Area 51 in Nevada is home to space alien captives. There will always be tall tales and we will always be fascinated by them but social media and our divided times have brought all of this to frightening, dangerous levels.

Besides the immeasurable damage of the QAnon nonsense, conspiracies abound about the vaccine, the virus, the deep state (whatever that is).

There are people who believe the vaccine includes a chip that allows the government to track them (Microsoft's bazillionaire Bill Gates is blamed), that the government is prioritizing illegal immigrants over citizens, that a vaccine passport will compromise personal security, that masks don't work.

Awhile ago the Alliance for Science published an article: *COVID: Top Ten Current Conspiracy Theories* (special note of the word "current," since it's a moving target). The list ranged from "COVID-19 Doesn't Actually Exist" to "COVID as a Plot by the Chinese or Big Pharma."

So many more but the common threads are fear and distrust. We are all exhausted from the disinformation which has become a cancer to democracy. Leaders in the government and the media know they are being deceitful but it serves their purpose. Liars like Fox News's Tucker Carlson and Sean Hannity, desperate politicians like Mitch McConnell and social media CEOs like Mark Zuckerberg are allowing it—even bolstering it. It is about power and money and fear.

I wonder if we can find our way back—with or without a global pandemic.

Day 389: April 7, 2021

I previewed another house for my kids today. Not a good option. Too remote. There is no housing inventory in San Diego and the homes that are available are hitting ridiculous prices. I'm secretly terrified that this whole notion of relocating to San Diego will be discarded when they struggle with a purchase.

Day 391: April 9, 2021

The Governor of Florida, Ron DeSantis, is suing the Center for Disease Control, demanding that cruise ships be allowed to operate. "We don't believe the federal government has the right to mothball a major industry for over a year, based on very little evidence and very little data." Someone needs to sit young Ron down and read him the un-fairytale of the Diamond Princess which quarantined her 3711 passengers and crew in February of 2020, when over seven hundred people became infected with COVID and fourteen died. It's non-fiction and the first in a long series.

Day 392: April 10, 2021

Prince Philip has died. He was ninety-nine and had been married to Queen Elizabeth since 1947. We have known Prince Philip our whole lives. He was the tall, sure fellow standing next to the Queen of England and now he is gone.

Day 393: April 11, 2021

It's Sunday again. Fifty-seven weeks of shutdown, so that must mean, roughly, fifty-seven Sundays. A few entries ago I went crazy trying to figure out if my "Day" count was correct. I was off by 100. That's how it is now—give or take a few weeks. But damn if Sundays don't show up over and over and way ahead of schedule.

And fifty-seven weeks in, we're still having debates about everything. Everything! We debate vaccines, of course. Will there be enough? Will we beat the variants? Will they work? Will the anti-vaxxers overwhelm us? Will we move into a "Fourth Wave?"

We debate immigration. Biden's compassion is what we asked for but it comes at a price. Unaccompanied children are overwhelming the borders and there are no easy answers for anyone—for the children, the parents, the communities, the enforcers, the social workers or the politicians. Biden promised to tame it and it may be his undoing. It is sure to be his Achilles heel.

I'm not done with debates but a short aside: The term Achille's Heel references a weakness or vulnerability. Rooted in the myth of Achille's mother dipping him in the River Styx, for protection, his entire body became invulnerable except for the part of his foot where she held him—the proverbial Achilles Heel. Worth mentioning.

The debates—yes… We debate the spending. We've raced past millions and billions. Trillions is the standard—an amount that defies comprehension. Congress agreed to $1.9 trillion in the COVID Relief package, and now we debate an additional $2 trillion for infrastructure and jobs. Few of us—Democrats or Republicans—know what's involved, but almost all of us have an opinion about whether that's enough, not enough, or just right. Goldilocks had it easy.

The most relevant debate, for now, is how, when, where, and what "opening up" should look like. We just moved into the Orange Tier, having suffered though Purple, then Red, then Purple, then Red.

Orange is new to us. Fifty percent seating in restaurants. Bars that don't serve food can reopen—although most had just figured out an easy food to serve, gyms, churches, museums, even roller coasters can increase their capacity and retail stores are now wide open.

Schools—almost. Big debate! Last spring, we heard an expert at the San Diego Department of Education talk about what would be needed to open up, and it was overwhelming. The distances, sanitation practices, personal hygiene, busing, personnel issues—it all defied any scenario that could work. On Monday, after thirteen months, San Diego Unified will open to 97,000 students, offering a hybrid of in-person and virtual learning. Of the 5,000 teachers, only 102 have sought a hardship exemption. Some hearty debates remain about spacing (three feet or six?), staffing (one or two per classroom?), days (make-up or just move on?). There are few clear answers about any of it including this: how will the children feel when they finally return and face each other and themselves?

Mirabel is so ready for pre-school. She is bright and has had remarkable tutelage through this time with her nanny and her parents but that social component of "playing next to if not with" will launch her into a bloom that will be magical. Her 2020 was a blessed version, but still isolated. I think about last summer's visit and our outings where nothing was more fascinating to her than another child, whether in a stroller or at the beach. The giraffes at the zoo held no interest to her if a fellow toddler toddled nearby. That very real need has been felt by people of all ages in this strange year. We long for others—even others we have never seen. Maybe it's a DNA or a God thing, who knows? But it's real and a year of pandemic demands that we acknowledge it.

In our COVID-ravaged world, we are beginning to experience the other side, sort our experiences, massage our scars. I've gotten better at the Sunday Jumble, but it's all still one tough puzzle.

Day 394: April 12, 2021

I have a folder in my desk drawer marked "Calendar"—a faded purple file that has held commitments of every stripe for more years than I can count. A coming-up folder that's known invitations to birthday parties, weddings, showers, RSVPs for galas, tickets to a play or a concert, meeting schedules, save-the dates, airline flights. This tattered file has held plans for great adventure and social commitments through many years.

I just opened it to find cancelled tickets to the Globe, the Pops and the sites in Barcelona that should have happened in May. I found a lockdown schedule for senior hours at Trader Joe's, Ralphs, and Target. But today, for the first time in a year, I put something fun into that tattered file— four tickets for the Flower Fields Tour and Jug Band music on April 25th. Now I just need to remember that that's where I put them.

And so it begins…

Day 396: April 14, 2021

Yesterday was exhausting. Just one hug after another!

A change, to be sure, and a welcome one with more loving embraces than I received in the last twelve months combined. I'm in awe of it, really, and so aware that each one was a gift. First hug was Alicia's in the morning—a last-minute visit with one of my favorite women in the world. The greeting at the door was familiar, "I'm vaccinated. Are you vaccinated?" That's the cue for the mask tossed and the embrace… well…embraced. Our sweet, animated visit ended with another brisk squeeze. I like those, too.

I got to friend Katie's and we did the same "I am… are you…" dance and then we hugged, a longer hold for Katie because life is hard and mean right now. Her dad, one of the great hug lovers of all time, is trying so hard to slip away and can't quite manage it. For my friend, it's been a long, quiet, lonely year. A hug can't fix that but it can make it hurt less for just a moment.

In the afternoon, I went to Nancy and Mark's to drop off my four-inch vase of roses. At Mark's direction, Nancy's birthday was celebrated with a caravan of friends delivering bouquets of love and beauty to someone precious we have already begun to miss. Nancy's journey with glioblastoma will end soon and Mark wanted her, on her last birthday, to view a field of flowers out her window. I had the privilege of a brief conversation and a loving hug with this dear man, an embrace of heartache, empathy and support. I hope his day held many from loving arms—something for him to bank in the sad days ahead.

And then, in the evening, hugs from four friends whose years of sharing, all tallied, approach triple digits. Barbara, Jill, Susan—we are all so different, but we share an understanding of how hard this year has been, how precious our friendships are and how fragile life can be. Barbara was sixty-seven yesterday. Susan will be sixty-five on Friday. Jill, our little sis, is only sixty-one. They whine and choke on the sixty part. I am their grateful den mother, at seventy. I'm okay with that—my elder status earns me a longer hug from these women I love.

No matter how long I live, I will never miss handshakes. They always felt like a test that had to be passed. And I will be grateful if I never, ever give an obligatory hug again—the hug you share with everyone you sort of know at the fundraiser or the hug you sacrifice when someone leans forward at a gathering and you realize you've got no choice but to lean in also.

Hugs—real hugs, bear hugs, heart to heart hugs—are like the perfect martini or a slice of mud pie or cool ocean air or finches at my patio feeder.

Except better.

Day 399: April 17, 2021

Prince Philip was buried today. Thirty people attended. His wife of seventy-three years sat by herself in the pew, nestled in a corner, entirely alone. She wore a black suit and hat, a black mask, and pearl earrings. That photo will be a heartbreaking and enduring image of the time of COVID.

Johns Hopkins University today announced the official global death toll of three million from COVID-19. The Associated Press wrote that the actual total is believed to be higher based on suspicions that many countries are underreporting infections and deaths.

Day 400: April 18, 2021

I lit a yahrzeit candle for my best friend, Martha, this morning. It is the 400th day of living with COVID. It is our fourth year of living without her.

Such a long short time.

I have thought of Tita (her South American name) so much this year because I always do but also because she would have helped us navigate this lost year. A north star, a moral compass, a guide. In her quiet way, she would have led by example with calm and comfort, from the first of the lock-down to the masks to the vaccine. Her politics would have held some fire and fierceness, to be sure, but she would have shown us all how to have those conversations without losing our kindness and without sacrificing our passion.

She would have found ways that no one else thought of to cheer the grandchildren she adored and to help the niños she served. She would have checked in with people we didn't think to comfort. She would have relished the quiet gifts that most of us failed to notice. She would have reminded us to laugh and to breathe when we needed it most.

"May her memory be a blessing."

It's a familiar phrase in this pandemic year. It's a Hebrew expression, almost a prayer—zichrona livricha—that has transcended the Jewish tradition to be shared by many faiths. Conveying hope, honor, grief... at once universal and intimate. A wish and a command. It recognizes the warmth and joy of a life now missed and gives us a chance to remember that that life lives on through our memory and deeds.

Martha held that kind of power for those of us who loved her. She made our lives and our world better. She was the example. She still is. I just wish we could have had her longer. Memory will have to serve.

May her memory be a blessing.

Day 404: April 22, 2021

I took a long walk around the neighborhood and saw not one, not two, but three banners that read, "Finally Open!" It's happening, at least here. India yesterday hit an all time record for one day cases reported—314,835. We need to remember that this is global, and the globe is still in great pain.

Day 405: April 23, 2021

I've looked at two more houses for J.T. and Kate. They made an offer on one of them. Got outbid. It's becoming a pattern of disappointment. Hopes up. Hopes dashed.

Day 406: April 24, 2021

Nothing.

Day 407: April 25, 2021

Yesterday, I wrote the date. That was as far as I got on a journal entry. Day and Date. I stared at my screen for a fair bit of time, thinking of all the things I've wanted to write about and yet, I wrote nothing.

I wanted to write about Officer Derek Chauvin being found guilty on all three counts in the death of George Floyd—a staggering relief of justice and a guaranteed shift in civic reaction, destruction, and discourse. As they read the verdict, hands all over the country, including mine, were raised with a triumphant, "YES!" It was a stunning moment and, we can hope, a tipping point of sorts. Certainly, George Floyd's death changed our summer of 2020 and perhaps our lives forever.

But I didn't write about that yesterday and I don't have the interest in giving it its due even now. I wanted to tell the story about the seventeen-year-old girl who, with her phone, videoed the whole long episode of George Floyd's murder after sending her little cousin into the store for ice cream.

Darnella Frazier wasn't trying to win a TikTok moment. She was just a young girl who saw something terribly wrong and could do little to help but understood that at least she could document. That made all the difference.

I wanted to write about police reform and the conversations we are having that may lead to some positive changes. Carotid Restraint is now banned. Police oversight commissions are forming. For all the absurdity of the notion to "Defund the Police," a thoughtful question is being asked and thoughtful people are trying to find answers.

I didn't write about any of that yesterday or the day before or even on April 20th when the verdict was announced.

I just didn't feel like it.

I've had more and more of those meh moments. Not hopeless, not inspired, somewhere in the foggy middle. I've been saying things like, "I'm just not interested" or "I've got inertia" (which I'm pretty sure is the wrong word), or "I'm so lazy." I may not be inspired but I'm also not lazy. "This isn't like me" has been my question, asked in the form of a conviction. WTF is going on?

A column in *The New York Times* gave me a hint. "There's a name for the blah you're feeling," wrote Adam Grant. "It's called languishing."

That's it! I'm languishing…I absolutely am! And those who suggest that giving something a name makes a good first step, well, I'm with them. I've been languishing and now that I know it, I feel better already.

But it's not all forward from there. According to Grant, an organizational psychologist at Wharton, it can be the first step toward some serious mental health challenges. He describes mental health as a spectrum from depression to flourishing. Despondency and despair on one end, thriving with a great sense of meaning on the other. Languish, he says, is the "neglected middle child of mental health" somewhere between those poles. An absence of well-being.

Let's be honest—this whole year made for an absence of well-being. A universal, tortured, physical, mental, political, social, educational cluster-fuck of unwell being. Some of us may never recover and all of us will bear scars. Well-being is a relative term.

This last year has beaten us all up. My wounds are mostly from the "missed experience" sort—that dream trip to Barcelona, more time with my kids, a chance to see the Northern Lights. I have not endured tragedy that is irreconcilable like death or violence. This year has held so much of that for so many and I know—truly know—how lucky I am.

Even without tragedy, we have all experienced profound emotions. We know them by name. Grief, loss, worry, loneliness, gratitude, relief, confusion. Complex experiences we could identify even as they washed over us. Even as they overwhelmed us. Even as they missed us.

With all of that in my mind, the word "languishing" is a gem of a gift. Now that I have a word, I know that I'm not alone with it, and I can begin to carry it with me toward the flourish side. I'm going to put it in my pocket where it can languish—another reminder that this too shall pass.

Day 412: April 30, 2021

Our grocery store has a new section. Not expanded produce or added liquor or a deli addition. In front of the pharmacy there is a large and loud collection of lime green patio chairs, spaced just about six feet apart and above it is a cheery looking sign that reads, in bold print, "THE COVID-19 VACCINE IS HERE." The graphics are a collection of brightly colored oranges. They seem to have nothing to do with anything. Maybe the fine print says, "Orange-ya glad?"

Yes. Yes, I am.

May 2021

*"It's amazing how a little tomorrow
can make up for a whole lot of yesterday."*

~John Guare

Day 414: May 2, 2021

J.T. sent a video of Mirabel singing. The tune is "This is the way we comb our hair, comb our hair, comb our hair…" but the words were, "I wish Mimi would come again, come again, come again…" So I shall, in ten more days.

Because I can.

Day 416: May 4, 2021

Disneyland has reopened. After thirteen months shuttered, the world's most famous theme park opened their doors just wide enough to welcome 25% of their guest capacity. If you must keep your mask on and you can't hug any of the characters and you don't get to have a parade or fireworks, is it still the happiest place on earth? Sure is. It's a magic thing.

Day 434: May 12, 2021

Liz Cheney, a Republican from Wyoming, is about to be ousted from her position of leadership in the House of Representatives. I don't agree with Ms. Cheney on much of anything except that Trump lost the election. One more difference between us, though, is that I can say it all day long and nothing happens. When she says it, she becomes a pariah.

I have great respect for her courage and conviction. "Remaining silent and ignoring the lie," Cheney says, "emboldens the liar."

Day 425: May 13, 2021

I'm not sure if we are becoming accustomed to the oddness or if it is becoming less odd. The sign on the seat beside me in the terminal read, "Please leave this seat open. More space to chill." Chill has a lot of euphemisms these days. The plane was still nearly empty. The hospitality bag was imprinted this time, but the contents were just as meager as they were on my flight in March. None of that matters.

As the driver pulls up to Mirabel's house, I see a sign in the window that has been crayon colored by a small child—a picture of emergency vehicles beneath a rainbow and above that, the words, "Thank you, New York." For four days I will see the oddness of Brooklyn, the quiet of the City and the joy of my family. Yes, thank you, New York.

Day 426: May 17, 2021

Glorious days with my little one and my bigger ones and my co-in-laws in New York. Mirabel's language skills are profound for her age and, thankfully, this time she issued no orders for me to go home. We played in the garden and did some cleaning up, which included an experiment to see just how much water her rain boots would hold. (Conclusion: more when her feet are not in them than when they are.) She has a wishing tree that she kisses as she walks by and a masked but otherwise naked dolly who accompanies her. When she poses for a picture, she says "Cheese Sabati" and she goes nowhere without her miniature pink Padre hat.

On the flight home, I stretched out in my row and thought about how soon I can return.

Day 427: May 18, 2021

The Supreme Court has agreed to take up a Mississippi law challenging Roe v. Wade. This is not good. This is really not good.

Day 434: May 22, 2021

It took moving to Washington, D.C. many years ago to make me appreciate the warmth of California sunshine. On a visit home after a tough winter, I told my parents, "You don't deserve all these flowers and blooms. In D.C., we've earned them."

I thought about that when we attended Marilyn's "Celebrate May" dinner party last night. Before this time, we didn't really deserve glorious evenings with enchanting tabletops, sumptuous meals, animated conversation. This fete had that and more. Her family is big fun, her tiered patio is a graceful space, the party favor was an odd and beguiling flower.

It feels like we have earned it.

Day 436: May 24, 2021

News about the economy keeps inching toward better, but it also keeps morphing in ways that continue to surprise. The slow recovery has put a brighter light on Work from Home (WFH) and asked new questions about the office buildings that sit empty—never mind the ones under construction.

We hear the phrase "The Great Resignation" often—it will assuredly be a book title, maybe even a movie, later on. Careers are no longer "hang in there for the gold watch" but "hang in there—or don't." Quitting, changing, retiring are the trend words and it's hard to know who's working hard and who's, you know, hardly working. Hustle doesn't mean what it used to.

The San Diego Union-Tribune has a regular column about side hustles that includes shopping for InstaCart and driving for Uber. Delivery is still the big daddy of side jobs but there's never been a larger demand for household repairs, homemade crafts, pet-sitting, or care for the elderly. Tech services are burgeoning and professional services offering freelance options, such as law or accounting, are filling another niche. Nine-to-five is becoming an antiquated notion.

The times they are a'changin'.

Day 440: May 28, 2021

My birthday. Seventy-one. None of the self-pity or fear or resentment of a year ago. Or at least a lot less. The carousel at Balboa Park has finally reopened, half of the adults in the United States have gotten the vaccine, our kids are still house hunting in San Diego and I got a video of Mirabel singing "Happy Birthday, Mimi" with a plastic bowl on her head and a big finish of "and many more!"

Yes, please.

Day 441: May 29, 2021

It's "the year after COVID" even as COVID remains our focal point for, well, all things. Traffic has resumed to "pre-COVID levels"—add that one to the *COVID Vocabulary list of words and phrases.* Masks still hide in all the corners of our lives—car, purse, garage, kitchen— and we still get halfway there before we remember to go back for one. Seventy percent of California's adult population have received at least one dose of the vaccine and *#CAComeback* is trending. All the improvised outdoor staging for restaurants is slowly morphing into permanent structures—an unintended consequence that should have happened without a pandemic.

San Diego had forty-five new cases last week and officials decried the efforts to dismiss their significance. *Keep the masks on. No big gatherings. Get the vaccine.* But we're becoming tired and sloppy, and we don't listen very well these days.

Add to that, an abundance of fools far and wide. Anti-maskers. Anti-vaxxers. And people who only step up for the shot when an incentive is offered—a lottery scratcher, a fast-food cheeseburger, or childcare. California just awarded $116 million in prize money with a top take of $1.5 million, all to convince you to get a vaccine that may save your life.

We've gone from begging for shots to begging folks to get them. New York is offering college scholarships. Ohio has a "vax-a-million" contest. God, America, just get the damn shot!

Many still believe the shot is not safe. *It was rushed. It was insufficiently tested. More harm than good.* Pro and con generally align with the political chasm which feels deeper and wider every day.

Part of this resistance is based on information from a U.S. database designed to track vaccine results. According to *National Public Radio (NPR),* the *Vaccine Adverse Event Reporting System,* or *VAERS,*

...includes hundreds of thousands of reports of health events that occurred minutes, hours or days after vaccination. Many of the reported events are coincidental—things that happen by chance, not caused by the shot. But when millions of people are vaccinated within a short period, the total number of these reported events can look big.

This is a long way of saying that the results of the initial vaccines were skewed by the population that was receiving it—those already at a high-risk with age or physical conditions so their mortality rate, with or without the vaccine, was disproportionately higher. But the numbers were the numbers and without the details, it just looks as if the vaccine was followed by death for many, to those who want to see it that way. In other words, it was because that population was nearer to death than those whose vaccines followed.

Cause and effect through a distorted lens.

June 2021

"*We do not remember days, we remember moments.*"

~Cesare Pavese

Day 446: June 3, 2021

In a year of weird weeks, this one scores high at our house. If the official kick-off of summer, Memorial Day, is a bell-weather, we're screwed. Mostly. And oddly.

On Monday morning, May 31, Memorial Day, Marty woke up with a puffy hand. Puffy like a glove blown into a balloon puffy. He felt fine. Cleaned the patio while he waited for his doctor to call back. We've got six close friends coming for a summer launch. It's a basic BBQ—burgers, dogs, chips, and some little flags stuck in anything a toothpick can secure. We're festive.

The doctor isn't happy about the hand so Marty heads up to Urgent Care to meet him for a look. No big deal. I'll stay and finish cooking and sticking little flags in stuff. When he called a few hours later, it was to say that he'd been admitted for blood tests and observation. Our friends, being good friends, managed the grilling and clean-up and eventually saw themselves out. I spent the evening at Scripps Clinic waiting with Marty.

Four days later, he's still there.

Marty describes himself as the healthiest patient in the whole hospital which may be true, but it would be nice if the labs could identify and confirm that. We suspect an infection of some sort or another. Mysterious but painless. Harmless or fatal. Don't know. So he waits for the labs and tries to bring cheer to a war-weary staff that has survived an extraordinary year. He's on the floor previously known as the COVID Ward. If these walls could talk... I just don't want them talking about Marty.

Day 447: June 4, 2021

Marty is home with a massive bandage on his hand, a face full of whiskers, and no idea what caused us to miss our Memorial Day party. We'll take the win.

Day 448: June 5, 2021

A cartoon in The New Yorker shows a line of people with one hand on the edge of the mask and a caption counting down, "Ten! Nine! Eight!…" Above them are balloons and a banner that reads: "Bottom of the Face Reveal Party!"

Day 453: June 10, 2021

The U.S. is buying 500 million doses of Pfizer vaccine to donate to other countries. That kind of announcement wouldn't have surprised my parents. It would have been a given for America to step up and share resources. But this isn't my parent's America. The Democrats are yelling that it's not enough and the Republicans are yelling that it's too much and then it births notions like "vaccine apartheid" (hoarding the medicine) and patent pushback (not sharing the formula).

Meantime, a nutcase pharmacist in Wisconsin just got a three-year sentence for intentionally destroying 500 doses of Moderna. Police said he believed that COVID-19 vaccine was not safe for people and could change their DNA.

Sigh.

Day 458: June 15, 2021

San Diego is "Open." That's a big deal. A little scary, but big. We've moved to the Yellow Tier (most of us never figured out what this prism system meant but yellow is nice), which is two people with COVID out of 100,000. But the critical key is the "contagion spectrum" (add that to COVID Vocab list). What's that mean? If you're vaccinated, masks are no longer required. Indoor service at restaurants, limited to 50%, larger gatherings are allowed, museums can open.

Call it a soft opening with, we hope, a soft landing. *If we can behave.*

Day 460: June 17, 2021

A big display at the supermarket today with massive overstock. The sign read, "All hand sanitizers 50% off."

Day 463: June 20, 2021

Late-night TV host Seth Meyers broadcast from his studio this week. That doesn't sound like much of a headline but for the last many months Seth, along with Stephen, Trevor, John, James, Jimmy, and Jimmy have all been doing their comedy shows from home. It makes a laugh line a lot harder for them and all of us. Humor is funnier when it's shared.

Trevor Noah rebranded his show as *The Daily Social Distancing Show*. Jimmy Kimmel cut his program to a half hour, tagged it *Jimmy Kimmel Self-Quarantine* and used his children's art for graphics. One of his earliest lines in his mini-dialogue: "You learn a lot of things when you are isolated. For instance, I learned that I have two young children. We made macaroni necklaces yesterday. Today, we ate them for lunch."

John Oliver broadcast from what he called the "white void space." Most of James Cordon's shows were shot in his garage. Jimmy Fallon was in his music room where his wife ran camera, his daughter played the piano, and his first guest was his dog (a beautiful golden, BTW).

Stephen Colbert has been our choice most nights and if we don't stay up for him, we tape the show. We've watched him get better and have become fans of his wife, Evie, who was his sole audience early on and an adorable presence. His humor is sharp, and his barbs are wicked. He spares nothing in full-throated criticism of Trump.

Mostly, what these hosts have all brought us is a sweet sense of togetherness. As Colbert said in a program early in the pandemic,

"America, you've been practicing for this your whole life. All those events you canceled, every two a.m. television binge, every Grubhub order from a place across the street. It was for this! Yes, we put a man on the moon, but, Yes! We're also the country where twenty-five million of us stayed home to watch it on TV. America, you got this!"

They're all back in their studios now. A milestone.

Day 467: June 24, 2021

We made plans to fly to Oregon to see Tom and Lisa—and we actually got to go! We used to worry that something rare would prevent a trip. Now we wonder if something rare will allow it to happen.

Tom and Lisa, our best of friends, moved to Sisters, Oregon, in the middle of the raging stage of COVID. Everybody, including them, thought it was crazy but it worked out well and we finally got to see how well. A warm and spacious home, lush grounds with wild flowers and pine trees, a serene mountain view and an honest-to-goodness barn for their horses. Everything about their new homestead feels and looks and smells like a change of direction. Like many people these days, they took a hard look at what they wanted and went for it.

COVID has caused many folks to recalibrate—if they can. Simply wanting to go for it doesn't mean you can go for it. Another economic chasm.

Day 471: June 29, 2021

We've made it through forty-three years together and that doesn't even count two or three of the courtship. Last night, it was time to celebrate, and we did it with a lobster fest and riotous efforts by our guests to eat them. Marty, from Maine, grew up with the crustaceans as a mainstay, so pictures were snapped when he held his master class in the proper method of steaming and cracking.

Our wedding, in 1980, included only a few more people than those counted in last night's celebration. Most of that group is gone now—people I miss every day. Marty's folks, my folks, even close friends. It's the hardest part about being older, I think—recognizing that those dear ones are gone and you are the dear one on the platform.

Gotta make this time count. As preposterous as this time is—it's what we've got.

July 2021

"Everything will be okay in the end. If it's not okay, it's not the end."

~John Lennon

Day 475: July 2, 2021

We made another plan to travel and travel we did! If Oregon was a breath of fresh mountain air, Durango, Colorado, was Rocky Mountain fresh times two. Cindy and George have a cozy and welcoming ranch house by a rolling river tucked in the woods where deer and bears are the main population. Heaven!

Alicia and Charles were there, too. I've shared board seats on non-profits with Cindy and Alicia, and I'm always wowed by the dedication, intelligence, and tenacity that they bring to making the world better. Add to that, they are wonderful fun. For four days we cooked and laughed and hiked and read and laughed and made S'mores and cooked some more and laughed some more. Our fellas enjoyed each other, usually from the patio chairs and between naps. We had bounties of food, lovely conversations, and times of gentle wonder with camp fires and starry skies. For a few days, with silly light-up Fourth of July eye-glasses and trips into town to browse art galleries, we got to forget what a mess the world is right now.

Cindy found an exquisite Apache mask for the fireplace wall. And then we found the right Apache prayer for this time and place:

Looking behind I am filled with gratitude.
Looking forward I am filled with vision.
Looking upwards I am filled with strength
Looking within I discover peace.

Day 483: July 10, 2021

Fully vaccinated teachers can take off the damn mask! The CDC says so.

Day 487: July 14, 2021

The Delta Variant seems to be making its way across the U.S. The only states not reporting a surge are Maine, South Dakota, Iowa, Delaware, and Arkansas. Missouri, which has the lowest vaccination rate in the country, has the fastest growing outbreak. There are no coincidences.

Mirabel has taken to wearing her mask low and her sunglasses tucked into her dress. Her curly haired image is usually finished with a backpack. My little two-and-a-half-year-old is a girl with style.

Day 493: July 20, 2021

It's baaaack…. Again. Damn!

Remember my friend, Nancy, an MD, MPH, who sent a note at the start of this mess outlining what might happen—all of which did, in fact, happen? We've benefitted from her friendship and expertise through all these months, and she's been upbeat and positive when the times warranted. Today's email subject: "Put those masks back on."

She describes this warning as "…not full hunker-down-and-go-nowhere-Instacart-time," but says we need to pay more attention. "The Delta variant is really scary, and we are seeing breakthrough symptomatic cases among the vaccinated, even though hospitalizations are not nearly as high. This is because it's affecting younger people with fewer underlying conditions." She goes on to say that the Delta variant is more infectious, high vaccine coverage doesn't entirely interrupt transmission, and with people still getting symptoms, the risk of long-haul COVID is real and can cause months or more of rapid heart rate, long term loss of smell and taste, and even brain fog.

We've been hearing about "Long COVID" for a few months but it's just now being recognized as a disability under the American's with Disabilities Act. According to the CDC, people who experience Long COVID most commonly report:

1. *Tiredness or fatigue that interferes with daily life*
2. *Symptoms that get worse after physical or mental effort*
3. *Fever*
4. *Difficulty breathing or shortness of breath*
5. *Cough*
6. *Chest pain*
7. *Fast-beating or pounding heart*
8. *Neurological symptoms*
9. *Difficulty thinking or concentrating (sometimes referred to as "brain fog")*
10. *Headache*
11. *Sleep problems*
12. *Dizziness when you stand up (lightheadedness)*
13. *Pins-and-needles feelings*
14. *Change in smell or taste*
15. *Depression or anxiety*
16. *Diarrhea*
17. *Stomach pain*
18. *Joint or muscle pain*
19. *Rash*
20. *Changes in menstrual cycles*

I can ignore number 20 but I just found 19 excellent reasons to mask up and try very hard to avoid this sucker.

Day 497: July 24

The Tokyo Olympics opened last night and, like all things this year, it was different. For starters, it was supposed to be last year, it was supposed to be attended by thousands, and it was supposed to open with upbeat music, jubilant athletes and cheering crowds. The only thing on that list of supposed-tos was the athletes. The Parade of Nations was vaguely familiar as uniquely uniformed but uniformly masked athletes waved to thousands of empty stadium seats. For their best efforts to welcome the world, the Japanese could not entirely mute the cries of protestors outside as the eternal flame was lit.

It's been eleven years since Marty and I had a grand experience volunteering at the 2010 Vancouver Winter Olympics. As part of the ONS (Olympic News Service) team in Whistler, we interviewed shy but determined athletes, sat through press conferences in languages we couldn't understand, and made our way through snowstorms and mazes of security in our turquoise "Smurf" uniforms. It was a time of adventure and awe.

We watched the tempered and sometimes solemn ceremony last night questioning, as many have, the wisdom of this event at this time but also grateful for the magic it might produce for a world that would dearly love some moments of magic.

Day 498: July 25, 2021

Pinch me! After five offers where they were outbid, I think our kids have found a house and I think it's here in San Diego and I think I'm going to be a ten-minute drive away from my granddaughter and I think Mirabel will go to a San Diego pre-school and I think I'll fix them dinner sometimes and I think I'll get to babysit and I think this is actually going to happen. OMG OMG OMG!

But I don't want to get my hopes up just yet…

Day 501: July 28, 2021

The U.S. House of Representative began hearings yesterday on the events of January 6. That day has been referred to by most as the day that Trump supporters stormed the capitol in an attempt to overturn the election. An insurrection.

This investigative body was intended to be bipartisan. It should have been bipartisan. So much needs to be learned about that day and the days leading up to it and the days following it that we should be looking through every lens available. But it turned into one more political football as appointments were made so that the group we have now is called "balanced" by one side and a "sham" by the other. It makes your head explode.

Yesterday's first four witnesses were police officers who defended the Capitol on the 6th. One called it a medieval battle that his Army and police training hadn't prepared him for. The horrors they each recalled were stark reminders against the revisionism that some Republicans have been spinning as if a group of tourists had happened into an unlocked building.

Liz Cheney, one of two Republicans appointed to the committee said, "I have been a conservative Republican since 1984 and have disagreed sharply on policy and politics with all Democratic members of the select panel, but in the end we are one nation under God."

Interesting times behind and ahead.

Oh, and the CDC wants us back in masks again. All of us.

Day 504: July 31, 2021

I'm depressed. I just read the Billboard's 100 Top 10 and I've never heard of a single song. Not one! Butter? Good 4 U, Levitating, Stay? Sounds more like dog training or magic tricks. Sigh.

August 2021

"plus ça change, plus c'est la même chose"
"The more things change, the more they stay the same."

~Jean-Baptiste Alphonse Karr

Day 506: August 2, 2021

Florida's COVID is skyrocketing with 2,683 cases in a twenty-four-hour period, but their governor has announced there will be no lockdowns, no restrictions and no mandates. He'll be heralded as a hero by the right, even as he kills a bunch of them.

But my kids are still on track with their Bay Park house and I'm letting myself believe this may really happen. A local grandma. Wow.

Day 507: August 3, 2021

Simone Biles has the Twisties. Our gymnastic darling and Olympic star is in trouble.

The Twisties—a term known well by gymnasts but not at all by the rest of us—disconnects mind and body when the body is doing extraordinary aerial turns. Biles lost track of where she was in her spins and, in the process, lost track of all control. She was, literally, lost in the air.

Now, because we all love this petite Olympian, we all know about the Twisties and worry for her. It's more than mastering the skills, as she has done. It's about surviving the sport.

Day 512: August 8, 2021

Tonight, after two years, we went to The Pops! The San Diego Symphony is back in their chairs and I'm back in mine. It's my favorite San Diego thing to do, and this year it's happening with a gorgeous new acoustic shell and a certain sense of permanence. Construction time made possible by a pandemic. A silver lining.

The excitement was palpable. The volunteers were welcoming and gracious. The musicians wore formal attire and perfect posture. The sunset was gold and magenta with wispy clouds and a breeze that felt like heaven. It was perfect!

Perfect for a pandemic.

The usual calm, almost spiritual communing I have always felt when the music met the air met the ocean met the community—it never arrived. The extraordinary Gladys Knight, in fine voice and sparkly sequins, made her moves across the stage and I kept thinking, *these tables are too close together.* The waiter brought the fine wine and I thought, *he should be wearing a mask.* Old friends came to share a hug and I thought, *what are we doing?* Just the gentlest ripple of worry but constant, nagging, intrusive. Maybe we're hardwired now. I don't know.

This magnificent venue accommodated 3,500, allowing for COVID. Eventually it will seat 10,000. Will we ever want to be that near each other again?

As we herded out, we donned our masks. Much of the crowd did not. It made me wonder how much of the crowd has had the shot. Sometimes I imagine a blue glow that comes from anyone who has chosen to opt out of the vaccine. Seems only fair to the rest of us. One more us vs. them. I'm waiting for that time when the music will, again, simply soothe my soul and let me escape.

Day 513: August 9, 2021

The Tokyo 2020 Olympics that happened in 2021 held their closing ceremonies last night. In past years most athletes stayed to take part in this grand event, but this year athletes were required to leave the athletic village within forty-eight hours of their competition so the attendance, along with no spectators, was small. An article in Aljazeera this morning pulled together the recap:

The 16-day event had no in-person spectators. Over 11,000 athletes competed. There were seventeen world records broken in everything from rowing to weight lifting. Swimmers had the biggest medal haul. The U.S.

scored a total of 113 medals. *The Tokyo 2020 Committee reported that 30,000 COVID tests were administered each day and 382 positive cases of COVID were reported.*

Last night's theme: "Worlds we Share." Victories were celebrated on a big screen, but the evening shared a soberness understood by everyone there and at home. As the baton was passed to France for 2024, the Olympic flame was extinguished with a collective sign from us all.

Day 514: August 10, 2021

The Senate passed a one trillion-dollar infrastructure bill with nineteen Republicans voting for it. Governor Cuomo has resigned over allegations of sexual misconduct. Hospital beds across the country are filling up with COVID patients.

Again.

San Diego, along with most of the country, continues to spike with the Delta variant, fueled by unvaccinated people and misunderstood by almost everyone. Yesterday, 869 new cases were reported in the county. Masks are required. We're over-confident in some ways and over-cautious in others.

This "vaccine hesitancy" (add that to our *COVID Vocabulary list of Words and Phrases*) is becoming exhausting. The battle cry from our side: "What would it take?" and "Just get the damn shot!" So many news stories of death-bed-regrets amid continued defiance.

In a phone exchange with my cousin, the excuses were layered from the politics to the science.

Her: It's still experimental.

Me: Except for the 352 million doses that have been administered to date.

Her: Nobody knows what's even in it.

Me: Yes, they do. Here's the website.

Her: Have you looked at the America's Front Line Doctors site?

Me: You mean the totally discredited M.D.s with no firsthand experience in endocrinology?

Her: It's my body.

Me: Try that one with the abortion issue.

Her: They're trying to shove it down our throats.

Me: Yes, because we're trying to get rid of the fucking virus.

Ok, some of that is not verbatim but this conversation started calmly and ended with tears. Predictable and exhausting. I love her. I don't want her to get sick and die. It seems pretty simple to me. The two of us represent the spectrum of these times, and we're both entirely entrenched in our own beliefs. This woman—smart, educated, informed—drinks from an entirely different fountain than I do. It doesn't matter that we love each other, played dolls together and share a history. We believe the other to be bull-headed and dead wrong.

Scripps Health System just sent a note saying all health care workers will require vaccination as of September 30 and that no unvaccinated visitors will be allowed entry starting tomorrow. One hour later an email arrived from UCSD saying the same—in English and in Spanish.

I have a fantasy of a school playground from so many years ago. A long row of children with their arms linked ferociously together as they yelled to the other team, "Red Rover, Red Rover, let COVID come over!" With some irony, COVID would take some deep breaths and begin to charge the line. Will it hold?

Day 517: August 13, 2021

Our friends, Donna M and Ann Marie, are heading to Arizona. Marty and I hosted a small dinner party tonight to say, "We love you and goodbye."

Donna M was a video editor with Marty for many years at the station and is retiring as the manager of News Operations at NBC/Universal.

She's a big deal and she's racked up awards in everything from Women in Technology to National Association of Black Journalists. Tenacious, positive, kind, smart, and funny as hell, she's also a black woman married to a white woman.

I hope Arizona finds a way to deserve her in these bizarre times.

Day 522: Aug 18, 2021

California reports 65,093 COVID deaths and 4,112,267 cases. The state just announced proof of vaccination or a negative COVID-19 test is now required for anyone attending an indoor event of over one thousand people. That's according to the California Department of Public Health.

We have no plans for attending indoor events with more than one thousand people but I've tucked my vaccination card in with my driver's license and Visa.

Just in case.

Day 525: August 21, 2021

We just got a few new photos of J.T. and Mirabel hanging out in their Bushwick neighborhood. The backgrounds are graffitied and tired with dirty sidewalks and hanging wires. The four pictures show a man and his little girl making faces and snuggled up, happy and silly and sweet. But I see some sadness in my son's eyes. For all of Brooklyn's rawness, I know he loves this place and will miss its' energy, noise and spirit. It makes sense to leave; his child needs a softer place to land each day but he's already missing it and the joy he had here.

A mother knows.

Day 531: August 27, 2021

Over 100,000 people are hospitalized right now in the U.S. That's the highest number since last January. Biggest spikes are in Texas and Florida.

Damn Delta.

Day 532: August 28, 2021

The kid's house is still on track. Looking good on the local grandma front.

When I let myself imagine how it will be to live just shouting distance from Mirabel, I automatically go to thoughts about the kind of grandmother my mom was to J.T. She totally nailed it. Completely from his perspective and nearly completely from mine.

I think about how quickly she said yes anytime Marty or I needed her help. I think about how faithfully she made it to every game. She knew more about J.T.'s soccer and baseball and basketball and football teams than I did and she knew more of the fellow parents and fans. I think about the time that I picked JT up and Mom's eye was a little puffy. When I asked she said, "Oh, I caught a puck." Her garage had been converted to a hockey ring.

She adored her only grandchild and he adored her. She overstepped sometimes—I will try not to do that—but otherwise, she was pretty damn perfect. WWHD—What would Helen do? That will be the question I'll ask, and I've got a hunch that Mom will usually be there with an answer.

Day 533: August 29, 2021

I haven't worked in years. At least not the get-a-paycheck kind. But I sure remember that feeling. Whether it was the handwritten check from the college bookstore or the envelope that you picked up from HR, that moment carried a quiet excitement. Work done and rewarded. Those who have only known automatic deposit have missed out.

Work, and the compensation that goes with it, are a big topic right now. One more thing that has been turned on its head because of the pandemic. In March of 2020, streets emptied, malls closed, schools stayed shuttered. Cancelled housekeepers, curtailed food service.

"Essential Workers" became a household term and those designated as such became heroes. Briefly. *Were they the lucky ones or the unlucky ones*, we asked rhetorically. They were working because we needed them. They were at risk. We were grateful.

They worked in hospitals, grocery stores, airports. Even the free food distribution lines, long snaking rows of cars pulling up with a popped trunk, like a creature throwing its jaws open, were serviced by essential workers putting boxes in one car after another.

WFH—Work from Home—became the standard acronym for those lucky enough to work remotely. Zoom was the vehicle, sweatpants the dress code. An option ripe with potential abuse by some; a godsend for others.

Essential workers slowly found support as coworkers were called back to the force, albeit grudgingly and with a fair dose of fear. Complications with childcare or remote schooling have challenged families everywhere. The stimulus check brought simultaneous sighs of relief and reports of misuse. Our split-screen continues.

In all my neighborhood walks I've noticed the window landscape change. We started with signs that said "Closed," then moved to "Masks required. Please stay six feet apart." Next were signs that gave the limited or expanded hours but recently, almost everywhere, the signs say, "Help Wanted." Small cafés and big chains. Every employer, it seems, is short staffed. It's been going on for awhile. People aren't going back to work.

Why?

For many months Federal stimulus money has helped families with children and the unemployed. On September 6, next week, that support ends. Some argue that there's no motivation to go to a job that pays less than you can make sitting home. That argument is usually made with some level of contempt and often by those who have second, not firsthand experience with it.

But what's the real story? Will all those signs come down next week when the tap is turned off? Is it that simple? I don't think so. Three hundred dollars a week may be a lifeline or an excuse or—as most of the pandemic has been—a serious pause for those taking a hard look at what they've been doing and where they've been doing it.

Day 534: Aug 30, 2021

The last plane officially carrying U.S. citizens and soldiers left Afghanistan ground today after twenty years. It will be debated for twenty more and twenty after that. One president started it, two more continued it and finally, a fourth one stopped it. It was an ugly, messy and polarizing finish but it was a finish. Of sorts.

Heartbreaking images of people running alongside a plane, trying desperately to escape along with the servicemen. A harsh reminder of images from the seventies when we did an equally bad job leaving Vietnam. That time tore the country apart, too. I knew which side I was on but I was too immature to bring the passion it deserved. As long as my friends were safe—most had been blessed with low lottery numbers and were working to stay in school—I thought I was doing my part to put up a colorful poster that read, "War is not healthy for children and other living things." Part naiveté, part stupidity.

My dad, a decorated Marine, felt strongly that it was not a war we should be fighting. He kept two stickers on the back of his camper truck. They sat side by side. One was the Fourth Marine Battalion logo, the other the ubiquitous peace symbol. People would, from time to time, peel one or the other off. Dad was prepared for that. He kept a stack of replacements on his desk.

Afghanistan. Vietnam. Cambodia. The Middle East. Ethiopia. It all reminds me of another poster from those college days: *What if they gave a war and nobody came?*

Meantime, Hurricane Ida has made landfall in Louisiana: a category four storm with 150 mile per hour winds that slammed the state on the sixteenth anniversary of Katrina.

Hospitals in the southeast are running low on oxygen amid a new surge of COVID.

Here in California, a massive fire continues to move toward Lake Tahoe with only nineteen percent containment.

The death toll from an earthquake in Haiti last week has reached 2200.

War, Hurricanes, COVID, fire, earthquakes.

And if that's not enough to convince you that the world is about to end, Ed Asner just died. He was Mary Tyler Moore's News Director, Lou Grant—feisty, misogynistic, and adorable. He's the week's final tragic blow.

Day 535: August 31, 2021

My daughter-in-law, Kate, has arrived for her first in-person look at the house that she will make a home for her family. This smart, savvy young woman takes my breath away sometimes. As independent as I was at her age, I think I would have been overwhelmed by all the change she is facing and all the conflicting priorities she's juggling but right now her laser focus is on this place where her family will live beginning, we hope, next month.

She seems to love the possibilities of this house but she's set on having some deep contracting changes made during a time when it's difficult to get much of anything done by contractors. She'll do it, I have no doubt. I just don't know how.

She'll split one bedroom into two. She'll fence the pool. She'll change the wall colors and the tiles and the fireplace. She's tapped on walls so she's pretty sure there's some found space in there that can be retrieved for toy storage. She'll rework the closets and drop the counter so it's kid friendly. Her punch list is a spreadsheet that would scare most convention planners. Finally, in a state that doesn't know the term *mudroom*, she's set on creating one and I've got to admit, it's a damn fine idea. Laundry here, shoes here, book bags and lunch boxes here, dog food here.

My beautiful, pregnant daughter-in-law is nesting and I'm counting my lucky stars.

September 2021

*"Taking on a challenge is a lot like riding a horse, isn't it?
If you're comfortable while you're doing it, you're probably
doing it wrong."*

~Ted Lasso

Day 541: September 6, 2021

L'shana Tova. A good and sweet year—a wish for ourselves and for others.

I edited a sermon this week—for Rosh Hashanah. It's a mitzvah that a good Lutheran girl can do for her good Rabbi friend each year. At least that's how we think of it and then she reminds me that Jewtheran is not really a thing and that my soul is mostly on her team.

She's right, but Jewtheran describes my ambivalence and allows me a foot in each world. I can have a mezuzah on the doorpost and a Christmas tree in the corner. Does that make mine a house of confusion or of faith?

In this year of 2021—5782 on the Hebrew calendar—with a world in so much pain, I ask old questions through a new lens. What *do* I believe. . . or do I believe at all? Is it the conviction of faith or the companionship of community that I crave? It's a question I asked in my Lutheran confirmation class when I was thirteen, as a counselor at Camp Yolijewa *(Youth Living Jesus' Way)* when I was eighteen, as I coached my son for his Bar Mitzvah when I was forty-something, and as I pray at the High Holidays today. I am, at once, skeptical, grateful and ambivalent.

Lots of smarter people than me have struggled with this. My life, an uneven tapestry of Mormon, Baptist, Presbyterian, Lutheran, and Jewish, leaves me with a disparate set of skills. I can recite the Nicene *and* the Apostles Creed and still manage a decent Shema. But I still have the odd set of questions: Is there a right way? Is goodness enough? Do I have a religion or even a faith?

Questions, questions. . . *Such* a Jewish thing!

A new year full of new hope for a better world and better answers. I will dip apples in honey and pray, as best I know how, for a good and sweet year for me and for this upside-down world.

Day 545: September 10, 2021

"Our patience is wearing thin." That's what President Biden said as he announced two new executive orders requiring about 80,000,000 Americans to get vaccinated. All federal workers and all healthcare workers who have Medicare or Medicaid assistance. It even mandates that all companies with one hundred employees or more require vaccinations or weekly testing.

"If you break the rules, be prepared to pay—and by the way, show some respect," Mr. Biden said. He's not messing around.

Day 546: September 11, 2021

This date will always be one of reflection. We will relive the moments and the images and it will continue to be a collective ache for our nation. It was a day of death, disbelief, and destruction. It was a day that changed us.

I decided to spend this twentieth anniversary doing something of joy. Something constructive. A simple task.

Marty and I assembled a child's table today. It's solid, sturdy. I labored over the color and went with a modest beige. Nothing too cartoonish— the story should be about the small child sitting at the small table and not the lime or magenta or plum that was already there. When she uses those colors, they will be all hers. And she will be all mine.

Mirabel is coming!

Day 555: September 20, 2021

During a time when television is still a primary form of entertainment, at least for my age group, the Emmy's get some attention. Last year, these ceremonies were held virtually but last night the glitter returned, sort of.

The venue was changed from the massive Staples Arena in L.A. to an indoor/outdoor space. Everyone attending was required to show proof of testing negative within the last forty-eight hours and they were asked to wear masks if they weren't speaking on stage. But the presentations were made in an oversized tent with a lot of folks who knew they looked better without a mask.

Seth Rogen went off script to say what everyone at home was wondering. "What are we *doing*? They said this was outdoors. It is not. They *lied* to us".

The big show winner of the night was *Ted Lasso*. I don't know anyone who would argue with the fun Ted Lasso brought to our locked-down lives. The quirky characters, the heart-tugging story, and the whiplash-fast quotable moments were a gift. Ted's sweet, complicated character gave us a real rooting factor when there weren't enough rooting factors.

"I've never been embarrassed about having streaks in my drawers. You know, it's all part of growing up."

"I do love a locker room. It smells like potential."

"You say impossible, but all I hear is 'I'm possible.'"

My favorite: "Ice cream is the best. It's kinda like seeing Billy Joel perform live. Never disappoints."

Or maybe just "**BELIEVE**."

Day 559: September 24, 2021

My granddaughter has a brand-new big girl bed. It's in Brooklyn for now but will be in San Diego soon enough. Her folks made a logistically challenging but very loving decision to surprise her with it now so she can bring it with her to a new home. A familiar place to snuggle in a foreign land.

With almost-three-year-old exuberance, she pronounced it all as "very cozy" and explained that her soon-to-arrive baby sister's bed would fit right beside it. She assembled her blanket and her bunny, got all the pillows just so, and then, that night, wandered down the hall and crawled in with her mom and dad.

Day 564: September 29, 2021

I'm officially boosted. My third shot of Pfizer 301308A was administered at the grocery store. Tony, our pharmacist, has gotten cracker jack swift with these. We exchanged a few stories about his kids and my grandkids, I give him my left shoulder, he managed the shot and the Band-aid. He was wiping down the counter and my chair before the door closed behind me.

October 2021

"Home is what you take with you, not what you leave behind."

~N.K. Jemisin

Day 571: October 6, 2021

A few days ago, the US COVID-19 death toll passed 700,000 with daily deaths averaging 1900.

Mind-blowing numbers that have stopped blowing our minds. Seriously! Every single day 1900 families are experiencing the grief that goes with losing someone you love. The crisis is still very real, especially for those families.

But tonight, Carnegie Hall in New York City will reopen. It's been shuttered for eighteen months, and tonight the Philadelphia Orchestra will play Bernstein and Beethoven and Shostakovich and for just a few hours, the arts will return.

The book *Station Eleven*, by Emily St. John Mandel, chronicles a world-wide pandemic and the efforts to rebuild by the few who remain. This fictional bestseller has the usual good guys and bad guys but Mandel uses the arts—Shakespearian Theatre specifically—to show that when life is renewed, it cannot just be about getting by. The band of performers are called the Traveling Symphony and their motto is "Survival is Insufficient."

Tonight, with a backdrop of months filled with grief and loss, the music will envelope the audience at Carnegie Hall and remind them, in heart-pounding splendor, that survival is insufficient.

Day 583: October 18, 2021

Colin Powell died of COVID today. Conservatives want to cushion that with "complications from COVID," but fact is, if COVID wasn't here, Colin Powell would be—at least for a while longer.

He was a statesman, a gentleman, a black man, a Republican. Chairman of the Joint Chiefs and Secretary of State. His positive outlook and elegant manner always seemed beyond military and politic. "Perpetual optimism is a force multiplier."

He could have been president except for two things. He didn't want the job and he made a big mistake with the intelligence on the invasion of Iraq. A "blot" (his word) on his record. It was a biggie.

I thought he was magnificent and I'm sorry he's gone. To COVID.

Day 584: October 19, 2021

We are, finally, beginning to break loose. Last night I howled at the moon, without a mask and in the very good company of women. I find an immense comfort in being with smart, interesting, clever women, all handpicked by a hostess who chooses her companions well.

"Bring a dish to share," the invitation read, "sweet or savory." Sweet won. By a lot. A small tray of salmon and a bowl of grain salad and some celery filled with cheese squeaked by. Those three tasty, sensible offerings did little to balance the hot apple pie, screaming chocolate cake, lush pumpkin cobbler, sticky rich brownies, and cupcakes high with frosting. No contest.

We lingered around those offerings like schoolgirls at the punch bowl. This year has done much to make wonderful moments feel even more exquisite.

None of us gave any thought—or at least conversation—to the news that the Texas legislature is messing with Roe vs. Wade or that there is a new Delta variant called AY.4.2 (or Delta Plus) that appears to be more infectious or that we may have just given each other COVID.

Sometimes girls just gotta have fun.

Day 587: October 22, 2021

Today I prepared the fairy house. It's a small crawlspace under the stairs—a bit of magic left by the former owners. Their cat went through the perfect miniature arched wooden door with the wrought iron latch to have a rest. It takes some gymnastics for a grown woman to get into the other entry, but today I managed it and tacked pink glittery fabric high enough that opening the little door will only show shine and sparkle. I recommissioned a woven drink coaster for an entry mat and found some tiny flowers meant for a dollhouse to adorn each side of the door. The fairies will offer a respectable welcome when they leave notes and gifts for Mirabel. They have told me they want to start with a shell. A small, perfect shell.

Counting down.

Day 589: October 24, 2021

California parents are beginning to protest the child vaccination mandate. It's a scary time to be a parent and this year hasn't put anybody at ease, to be sure. But come on. When we were kids and lined up for the polio vaccine or the sugar cube—a particularly fond memory, nobody felt anything but grateful (okay, and briefly scared).

Parents who are freaked out that their children will have nightmares because they were made to wear a mask—well, my mind keeps going back to the iron lung that a friend of mine wore. Now, that shit was the stuff of nightmares!

Homeschooling student numbers have sky-rocketed during COVID. It's a natural extension of this shut-in time, but my years of teaching tell me that not a lot of these parents can really know what they're doing no matter how pure their intentions.

Worse, the pro and con camps seem to be breaking, as so many things do today, down political divides, which makes me wonder how much of the curriculum will be informed by the political beliefs, biases, bigotries.

Nothing is simple right now.

Day 592: October 27, 2021

J.T., Kate, and Mirabel are in San Diego. To stay.

Exactly thirteen years ago, in 2008, my son and only child flew to New York City where he would make his life, find his love, and start his family. It was exactly the right choice for him and one of the hardest moments, ever, for me.

Thirteen years later to the day, he has returned to San Diego with his wife, his child, and another due soon along with his new dreams to root (or reroot) in his home town. It was a joy to raise this kid and I love the man he has become. He still has a wonderful zest for life—a phrase we read on many grade cards—and it translates to his role as husband and father. I still don't believe they are here.

For them, it's a two-sided coin. With the family picture Kate posted on Instagram, it's clear that the joy to come does little to blunt today's pain of leaving. She's eloquent in her farewell.

"It was a bustling day as we packed our life in Brooklyn into a moving truck. Then, at the end, some quiet sadness as we said goodbye to a home that held us as we made some of our most important memories, and a community of family, friends, and neighbors that has lifted us up and made us feel safe and happy.

"New York City, the place where 'everybody's got a job/everybody's got a dream' (from Lin Manuel Miranda's 'In the Heights'). The place that gave me a sense of endless possibility, a career I love, the family of my dreams and so many relationships that have shaped me.

There's nothing like the feeling that you've made New York City yours: It's hard, it's gritty, it's beautiful, it's successful, it smells bad, it's the most driven collection of interesting/fast/brilliant people that I know. A mess of contradictions and perfect meanings, a work of art. A place that I will always feel both critical and protective of; like a sibling, like a home."

She ends her note with an invitation to her friends and apologizes for the *"novella-style softhearted post. Leaving the melting pot has melted me a bit."*

I must be mindful of her pain. They have given up so much with this move. Maybe they would have made this choice eventually, but COVID brought them to me sooner.

My kids are home.

Day 593: October 28, 2021

The FDA announced today that the Pfizer vaccine is approved for children ages five to eleven.

Day 595: Oct 30, 2021

I'm spent, whooped, knackered.

I went to bed at 9:00 last night. 8:00 the night before. All because of Mirabel.

A Marine just out of boot camp would not be able to keep up with my almost-three-year-old whirling dervish granddaughter. Muscles have been activated for the first time since I tried out for high school cheerleading. All the walking or strength training or visualization was not nearly enough to keep me from the industrial strength Aleve bottle and a shower that defied water quotas. But I'm making progress and as soon as I hear, "Mimi, let's do this…" I'm up and running!

Day 596: October 31, 2021

My little one wants to be a ghost and she wants Mom and Dad to be ghosts. They are a little ghost family. They will don white shirts and white pants, put on white face paint.

And white N-95 masks.

It's tempting to be glib and talk about a haunting year or mention the irony of a ghost family in a year that lost so many souls and spirits. But it's a day for treats and trickery, children and chills and skeletons and spiders. I think I'll just watch my ghost brood head out for their party and thank my lucky stars.

November 2021

"Often when you think you're at the end of something, you're at the beginning of something else."

~Fred Rogers

Day 597: November 1, 2021

My husband frets about the weather. He worries, it will be too cool—should he take a jacket or should we add a blanket to the bed? He worries it will be too hot—should he start with long pants or shorts? Where's his chill bandana? He monitors the details on the Oregon Scientific thermometer on his desk like nurses monitor a patient's blood pressure. It's just who he is and it's a large part of why we live in California.

But there's that bigger issue. The way bigger issue. The one with the global temps and worldwide weather related crises. The one that most of us don't want to think about.

President Biden is at the International Climate Conference in Glasgow, a 2020 event that had been postponed by COVID. The leaders hope to secure a commitment to steps that would hold the temperature increase to 1.5 degrees. Doesn't seem like much to ask (insert: smiley face emoji, wide-eyed face emoji, exploding face emoji).

I wonder if someday, someone—perhaps Mirabel—will be writing a journal about the changing climate and the impact it is having on life every day, relating the personal challenges that must be met and wondering how we got there. Like COVID on steroids.

It's a thought that makes me sad because no vaccine can combat climate change.

American Airlines cancelled 850 flights yesterday, partly because of weather. Mostly because of personnel shortages. The workplace is changing shape everywhere—high and low. One of the top selling items on Amazon right now is the Video Conference Lighting Kit with a ring light that makes you look just a bit more alive in all those Zoom meetings from home.

Not to get lost in all of this, the world just reached the five million mark of deaths directly due to COVID. Five million souls who were alive before this pandemic. Almost 800,000 in the U.S.

How is it possible that this much change and grief has not brought us all closer together?

Day 598: November 2, 2021

My family is scattered...
    Mirabel and Marty are at the park. Masked.
    J.T. is on a work Zoom on the balcony.
    Kate is at their house with the contractor splitting one room into two.
    I'm in the kitchen fixing dinner.
    Apart, then together.
    A matter of distance.

Day 600: November 4, 2021

J.T. and his family have moved into an Airbnb. They need their autonomy and it's a good half-way step before they can move into their San Diego maybe-forever home. Having five people and a dog in a space that became accustomed to just two was chaotic, but I miss them. Sometimes I think that the pioneer days with many generations under the same roof would have suited me. But there is something to be said for a decent night's sleep.

Day 601: November 5, 2021

We're all learning the Greek alphabet. There's Alpha, Beta, Delta, and now, Omicron. Evidently, we used to name viruses for their identified place of origin, but that proved unreliable and prone to stigma. So the World Health Organization (WHO) decided to use the Greek Alphabet. I guess nobody cares if Greece is stigmatized.

It seems like Omicron skipped to the front of the line, but I'm learning that variants were named for all the other letters, too. Epsilon, Zeta, Theta, Kappa, Iota, and Eta didn't amount to much (especially

IOTA. Get it?). According to WHO, the five variants of concern are Alpha, Beta, Gamma, Delta, and Omicron. Lambda and Mu are waiting in the wings.

It's enough to give the best fraternity a bad name.

Each new variant strikes fear as speculation trips all over itself. "Likely to be worse than the last one" and "…may be immune to the vaccine." We get smug thinking we know about what's been and what's coming, but the fact is, we don't know squat. We may be done, or we may be at the beginning…just as we start to let down our guard—and our masks.

Day 603: November 7, 2021

Oxford has chosen, as they always do, a Word of the Year. This year the word is VAX.

Elisha Fieldstadt, with NBC, noted that "anti-vax" showed up in the early 1800s, "Vax" dates back to the 1980s but it took the internet of the 2020s to give it full expression:

In the age of social media, vax led to words like vaxxie—a selfie taken while getting the COVID-19 shot, and vaxinista—a person who flaunts their vaccinated status by going out more and traveling more (taking vaxications).

Vax, shot, pop, jab. Boom, pow, wham, zap!

Day 605: November 9, 2021

The University of California, Berkeley, was supposed to play USC today but they cancelled after two dozen players tested positive for COVID. Most of these kids were vaccinated and are asymptomatic, but it was still enough to call it off.

A huge ripple is launched in a moment like this. Fans who would have attended just changed their schedules and their lives. Vendors and groundskeepers and cheerleaders and parents just got a schedule whiplash because a couple dozen kids have COVID.

Testing positive. Not a good thing. The new grading system.

Day 606: November 10, 2021

For the third time since last March, Gavin Newsom has extended the state of emergency for California. That will take us to the end of this March which means that we can mark a second anniversary for the state of the state. On March 4, 2020, Newsom declared the first emergency and memory of it is still haunting. Holding up a bottle of hand sanitizer, he announced that price gouging would not be tolerated.

His language today brought the same kind of chill. "Winter is coming," he said, invoking Game of Thrones. "Winter is here." Besides fear of the new variant, Omicron, there is this: winter brings us indoors and heightens exposure. For some extra high anxiety, he reminded everyone that the flu season, which didn't amount to much last year, looms over us as well. "We want to avoid the *Twindemic*."

No shit.

Day 608: November 12, 2021

I will remember tonight forever. I will remember the little dress she wore—primary color stripes with a crisscross top. I will remember the distance between us when it happened—maybe thirty feet. I will remember the way the floor looked in the family room—a slick tile that opened up to a flagstone patio that looked further to the pool and the ocean beyond. I will remember all of that as her backdrop but most of all…most of all I will remember her outstretched arms as she ran toward me calling, "Mimi!"

We haven't celebrated Shabbat for ages, but we have close friends who always do and tonight we were with them. It was a "Welcome Back!" Shabbat for J.T. and his family. The crowd was intimate with friendships that began when our boys were the age that their children are now. Irresistible food, mostly Persian and exotic but familiar for the many times we've enjoyed it together: fragrant koobideh with secret spices, polo with cherries and rice (a race to get the crunchy bottom layer), hummus and radishes—all textured and inviting.

Generation to generation—a treasured Jewish value—holding the past with the present, the elders with the children. The next generation of small children found echoing halls to run through, squeals to make and new friends to chase.

But that first scream I heard—the one with full volume and uninhibited delight—the one of such tender and boisterous recognition—still rings in my ears. I will pull it up when I need a lift. I will replay it when my three-year-old has become a difficult eight or insecure eleven or cocky fourteen. It will forever be the sweetest sound of my life, the purest sound of joy. My granddaughter was calling my name.

Day 609: November 13, 2021

The United States has reported more than forty-seven million cases of COVID but the headline in nearly every newspaper was "Britney Spears Conservatorship Terminated."

I think we needed a distraction.

Day 610: November 14, 2021

Today would have been my best friend Martha's seventieth birthday. I miss her.

I was thinking about her and our friendship and our gang and needed to write about the longing and gratitude I feel for these people who are such a part of me.

We were fifteen together and then twenty-five and forty-nine and seventy, seventy-one, seventy-two. We attended each other's weddings, divorces, hip replacements, milestone birthdays—twenty-one, forty, fifty, sixty. We have shared car shopping, car crashes, tequila shots, shingles shots. Our long conversations have been on the family phone, the princess phone, the mobile phone, the cell phone and, finally, on Zoom where we shared COVID fears and phases.

There is a ritual and there are rules that govern growing old together. It's an inexact formula, but there are three parts: Part one is reminiscing— tales of ditching class, raucous rock concerts, salty margaritas, romantic grad nights, career turning points, and crushing world events…the kind of world events that made you wonder if the world will go on. We talk about them. Turn them over in our minds and hearts. Take energy from each other to face the next big thing.

Part Two is questioning—How's the family, have you seen that old friend, that great movie, political mess? When did you get promoted, pregnant, discouraged, diagnosed, retired? How can I help?

Finally, Part Three is appreciating. This is the quiet part. It whispers about the moments we shared when he told us he is gay, or they told us they were expecting or she told us she was sick or they told us they'll be grandparents or they called to say she's gone. Together for the wedding or the funeral or the baptism or the bar mitzvah or the hospital visit. The loud moments dancing to brass horns. The quiet moments holding hands in neon-lit waiting rooms.

My high school gang has grown old and we have done it together. Now we gather at the beach each summer that the world allows. We are a picture out of a Simon and Garfunkel record cover. We laugh. We worry. We tease. We share.

Those shared experiences are only possible if the ones you shared them with are still here. Pour another margarita. I'd like to make a toast…

Day 612: November 16, 2021

We went to the zoo today. Not many masks amid the confidence that comes with being outside and wanting it to be okay. My granddaughter bounced as I walked and everything about her makes me feel lighter and happy.

When a disheveled orangutan came up to the window, she said, "Hello!" While the scrawny monkeys were swinging from one tree to another, she held a bamboo sculpture and tried to climb it. When the coral flamingos cawed and perched on one leg, she did, too.

A young boy in a stroller began to cry and she stopped to touch his hand and say, "It's okay." A tall boy, her age, challenged her to a run up the nearby ramp and she took him on. She's tender and fearless and always ready for whatever is next. Each time she returns to take my hand, and off we go.

Day 618: November 22, 2021

Those of us of a certain age will never be able to write *November 22* without a pause. It was the first time I would share a memory with the world. We all remember where we were, what we felt, what we thought it meant.

1963. I was at lunch between Civics Ed and Algebra 2. My friend Dee Cook grabbed my hand and told me that President Kennedy had been shot but she didn't believe it so we went to the pay phone and she called her boyfriend who was a delivery boy for the local newspaper. I don't know how it is that we could call him and why we thought a delivery boy would have the inside track, but I remember standing inside that pay phone booth with our dimes, our nerves, and our naive connections. I was thirteen years old and the world had just been rocked.

Many years later, as a high school teacher, I felt a jolt when I referenced that day and none of my students had any memory of it.

I'm thinking about this today not just because it is the fifty-eighth anniversary of JFK's assassination but because I wonder what shared memories we will have of COVID. Will a young woman remember her thirteen-year-old self and the hours that she stared at a computer screen during algebra, longing to be with friends? Will she know what "Civics Education" is? Will she remember the confluence of politics with COVID, civil unrest with social injustice? Will it be a memory about finding a cure or losing hope? Will she remember it at all?

Day 621: November 25, 2021 Thanksgiving Day

Grateful beyond measure. That's become my mantra since my kids moved to San Diego. On this day of thanks, I feel it so deeply that it moves aside the chaos.

I set a table that would make my mother proud with her fine Baccarat crystal, a purchase I've always thought foolish and still do. But she wanted those one hundred dollars per stem water and wine glasses so badly that she made it happen and now they grace my table along with the less elegant placemats and place tags and everyday flatware. The meal is traditional, ample, and quite fine, albeit with a little less butter and a lot more wine than the Thanksgivings of my youth.

My Jewish mother-in-law, never holding high expectations of my epicurean talents, always said, "It's not what you put on the plates. It's who you put in the chairs." She was right and we score high on that mark. Kate, J.T., Mirabel, of course. Kate's sister, Margo, is here and adds a bright glow. My darling Aunt Donna and her granddaughter Dani are a precious addition. Two very different generations who spent COVID doing puzzles together on FaceTime. They've chosen our table and I am honored. Also, if we talk politics, which we may or may not do, we will all be in alignment. It's an added calm in these troubled times.

Finally, as all good Thanksgiving tables should, we have a neighborhood orphan. Richard, who began as our physical trainer and has become a friend, had no other invitations and, lucky for us, accepted ours.

The President of the United States gave a Thanksgiving Address, as is the tradition. He thanked the doctors, the nurses, the scientists, the parents. Most of those people are not usually thanked in this annual speech. "We are grateful for the educators who are welcoming children back into their classrooms, helping them make up for lost learning and lost time, both academically and socially." I'm grateful for Joe Biden.

It's been a Thanksgiving of considered possibilities. Is it possible to travel? Is it possible to be with those we love the most? Is it possible to enjoy time with those same people? We are all quietly aware that COVID and distance are not the only things keeping this table limited to the parties around it.

Significant chasms that may keep our family, and families all over the United States, from celebrating a holiday together again soon. Us vs. Them, Red vs. Blue, vaxxed vs. unvaxxed, Trumpers vs. Never Trumpers. The divide is deep, wide, and very painful. Especially on a day of thanks.

It's not just about whether you call it stuffing or dressing anymore.

Day 623: November 27, 2021

Black Friday, the day after Thanksgiving and traditionally the biggest shopping day of the year, has come and gone. They're still tallying the impact but it's safe to say that more folks did their Christmas shopping on the couch than at the mall. Meanwhile, California marked its five millionth case of COVID, up from three million last January, four million in August.

Big spending shared the headline with Omicron, which the World Health Organization classified yesterday as a "variant of concern"—a label that indicates more virulence or vaccine resistance.

Santa Claus and Omicron are comin' to town...

December 2021

"You are braver than you believe, stronger than you seem, smarter than you think, and loved more than you'll ever know."

~A.A. Milne

Day 627: December 1, 2021

Time to pull out the *COVID Vocabulary list of Words and Phrases* and add "Supply Chain."

We probably should add "Ripple Effects," "Global Economy," "Unintended Consequences," and "Manufacturing Models," too. And "Labor Shortages," all part of product supply and international manufacturing. Right now, the words add up to a goddamn mess!

The shortages started right off the bat with toilet paper and masks and gloves. Basic supply and demand. Then the scarcity of ventilators became a genuinely frightening situation. We moved to refrigeration when the bodies (sorry) and then the vaccines demanded it. Next, and now, problems with life-sustaining products like food and medicine.

In a recent article in *The New York Times*, titled "How the World Ran Out of Everything," Peter S. Goodman and Niraj Chokshi describe a business model called "Just in Time" manufacturing which, simply put, meant that products were only produced as needed instead of stockpiled. It was a new approach, and it became a world standard—at least until a global pandemic—when "as needed" became "needed NOW!" In 2021, the Just in Time model has us by the global balls.

The most glaring example was the desperate shortage of safety equipment for the health care industry, but by now it's affected all of us, whether we've gone looking for paint sealer, tapioca, or a new car. As we've gotten used to not dressing for work, a shortage of athletic wear surfaced. As kids got used to staying indoors, a shortage of gaming consoles and iPhone 13s followed.

The next link of the chain is labor shortages. Products have been shipped but cargo vessels stay stuck in seaports. Shipping containers spend months in their harbors of calling. Labor shortages means no one to work the ports or drive the trucks that would carry the goods.

So here we are nearing Christmas, with a whole new batch of shortages like Christmas trees, Hanukah candles, and Tonka Trucks! Dear God, not Tonka Trucks.

One more word for our list: "Pivot!"

Day 630: December 4, 2021

The seventh night of Hanukah. We joined friends for crisp latkes and tender brisket, a cinnamon kugel and soft fragrant challah. With a promise of "all vaccinated," we shed our masks at the door and made a sweet night of traditions for everyone. Five children with five menorahs with seven candles lit on each one makes a glorious light. And then, because she will be three in three short days, a special cake with three candles came out to a surprised and slightly confused Mirabel. After sharing this warm evening, she shouted, "Happy Birthday, everyone!"

A candle's light and a child's joy. It gives you hope.

Day 633: December 7, 2021

Mirabel is three! It was a modest celebration but seemed just right for the time and place. Our three-year-old had adoring adults—her parents, the Steins, me, and Marty—posing under balloons in the shape of a butterfly and Paw Patrol's top dog, Chase.

They're still at an Airbnb so the spare kitchen with its limited equipment made birthday baking a challenge, but Kate is resourceful and the cupcakes were perfect. It took six tries but Mirabel never stopped until all three of those candles were out! If she forgot to make a wish, we all had plenty of them for her.

Day 634: December 8, 2021

NPR's Morning Edition did a story headlined "Pro-Trump Counties Now Have Far Higher COVID Death Rates. Misinformation is to

Blame." It's not an insignificant difference, this red vs. blue story. Turns out that the folks waving the "Don't Jab on Me" flags are three times more likely to die from COVID than those waving Biden flags.

The story says that partisanship is the single greatest predictor of whether a person will be vaccinated. Fifty-nine percent of Republicans have been vaccinated compared to ninety-one percent of the Dems.

An embarrassment of ironies (Is there such a thing?). Trump planted this seed, watered it with disinformation and then whined when he didn't get credit for the fruit. He rightfully brags about getting the vaccine developed with his Operation Warp Speed, but kept secret for two months that he had gotten the shot. How many lives might he have saved if he had just told the truth?

Day 639: December 13, 2021

Mask mandates are back.

Day 640: December 14, 2021

I ordered an assortment of child-size KN-95 tie-dyed masks for Mirabel, a large box of KN-95 whites for us. I hope that someday I stumble on some of these left over from this order and wonder why I never pitched them.

Vaccine scientists have been named "*Time's* 2021 Heroes of the Year."

Day 644: December 18, 2021

We danced at the zoo tonight—Marty, Mirabel, and me—and when the first mask got too sweaty and cold, we changed masks and we kept dancing. We rode the bus and dropped the mask long enough to smile for pictures. When we approached the Lemur section, Mirabel jumped into the aisle and demanded, "Okay, everybody together: 'Hakuna Matata'!" She brushed a giraffe as the bus passed by and came home with a monkey-shaped flashlight.

But not until we danced some more.

Joy to the World!

Day 645: December 19, 2021

A friend of mine has lived an especially solitary life since lockdown. She's single, fiercely independent, and creative enough to be outstanding as a college instructor using Zoom. But so alone. When we finally were able to get together, months ago, on the patio for a glass of wine and conversation, I asked, probably with pity in my voice, "How have you been?" She answered sheepishly, as if caught telling a secret, "I'm thriving."

Strange to think that this time, for some, has been a respite. A time when one's own expectations were the only expectations that had to be met. There's freedom in that. For most of us there has been some bad and some good. Some scars, some enduring blessings. Some spiraling and some thriving.

Marty and I have had one of the easiest assignments these twenty-two months. Retired with few demands that we couldn't meet, sometimes with an assist from Instacart, Amazon. Our job was to stay out of the way and not worry. I have been better at the first than the second. Stay out of the way and count your blessings. Keep your chin up. There's always a bright side. Look for the silver lining.

In times of war, those phrases end up in songs and poems and posters. In times of COVID, they haunt us for the perspective they demand.

According to Vocabulary.com, the term "silver linings" goes all the way back to 1634. "The origin of the phrase seems to be John Milton's

1634 poem 'Comus,' which includes the line, 'Was I deceived? or did a sable cloud Turn forth her silver lining on the night?'"

I like that. Elegant and subtle.

Americans are more about getting hit over the head when we talk about optimism, and we usually throw in a dose of melancholy and drama.

The wistful melody of "I'll be Seeing You" got many war brides through the loneliest times, or for more war stories, go back even further and listen, closely, to "When Johnny Comes Marching Home."

"The girls will scream and the boys will shout, The old folks too will all turn out…"

"Look for the Silver Lining" was a popular Jerome Kern song written in 1919 and made most famous by Judy Garland although her rendition oozed more melancholy than hopefulness.

Remember, somewhere the sun is shining
And so the right thing to do
Is make it shine for you.

The king of all of them, at least in modern times and my opinion, has to be Monty Python's "Always Look on the Bright Side of Life," as he hangs from a cross and whistles to the others being crucified. "Some things in life are bad, They can really make you mad" might be the simplest and most dead on anthem of the last many months. "When you're chewing on life's gristle/ Don't grumble, give a whistle…"

Since March of 2020, I've grumbled a lot, whistled a little, but always known how lucky I am so it's time to collect my list of bright sides and silver linings. I've been a list maker my whole life. Sometimes I write "make a list" on my lists just so I can have the immediate pleasure of checking something off the list.

But this list isn't for checking off—it's for checking in and measuring some of the bright lessons that have been part of a dark time, the reasons to stay optimistic and believe it will all work out. I've had a note stuck to my fridge since before this pandemic began. "Everything will be okay in the end. If it's not okay, it's not the end." Do I really believe it? Not entirely, but then again, it's not the end yet, right? And the fact is, this global pandemic has offered me some rare gifts:

Like: I began writing in earnest which led me to classes which led me to new friends. I will keep those friends and I will keep writing.

Like: I got a puppy, which led me to understand that my years as a dog owner are done. And that's okay. Dogs are tender taskmasters and I don't want to be at the mercy of one ever again. All that discovery led us to find the ten-out-of-ten new home for Poppy with a family that couldn't love her more. A silver lining for us and for her.

Like: I had a lot of time alone, which led me to realize that I really like time alone.

Like: I had a lot of time alone with my husband, which made me remember what a good and sweet man I found more than forty years ago and how lucky I am to have his company, kindness, and patience on this journey.

Like: I watched some very good television shows—*Schitt's Creek* and *Ted Lazzo* at the top of the list—and was surprised at what a sweet thing it was to look forward to each evening. That and ice cream and holding hands with Marty.

Like: I learned not to grocery shop so often which led me to realize that my freezer isn't the enemy.

They're not deep thoughts or profound lessons. I know that. Not compared to the lessons that many others had to learn, like how to cope with children who are expected to stare at a screen all day as if in a classroom. Or how to care for an elderly parent with resources that pale and patience that is waning. Or how to make a living when you're not "essential." The bright sides found by those folks are life changing.

On the global scale, some bright silver linings, like the speed at which a vaccine was developed and brought to the public. Or how resourceful we became in our ability to do virtual weddings, birthdays, and even funerals. How we all pitched in to make our communities work better. Crime rate went down, library check-outs went up. We learned so many ways to be "apart-together."

Finally, for me, one silver lining is actually gold. My kids realized that they could work from anywhere and that anywhere, right now, might as well be San Diego. I don't have to "know" my granddaughter through a screen. I can chase her in the yard, snuggle with a book, share butterfly kisses.

Silver and gold never shone brighter.

Day 646: December 20, 2021

Our son and his wife went to the hospital tonight. Kate is in labor.

They're settled into their second Airbnb, one that will accommodate her parents too, and will have their new home move-in ready very soon. But not yet. I stopped at the local garden nursery and found a slender tree because it seemed like a little girl and a baby girl and exhausted new parents should have a Christmas tree, albeit a scrawny one, on Christmas morning.

Kate's parents have arrived after an uneventful and fully masked flight. BarbaraJean will begin to fill the kitchen with wonderful smells of nutritious broths. Scot will tear into house repairs and make unworking things work again. But for right now, we only care about Kate and J.T. and Mirabel and the miracle that is our world today.

It's been nearly two years since our neighbors sat around a table laden with snacks and Corona Sunrise drinks and had our first real buzz-kill introduction to COVID-19. We weren't frightened; we didn't know enough to be frightened. It was almost exciting to think that this giant shared experience was about to happen. Like a bad storm forecast. It might get a few things wet but nothing to really worry about.

We were wrong.

It's still storming. Raging at times, calmer at others. A constant storm that no one is allowed to ignore.

But life goes on.

Day 637: December 21, 2021

∾ *Ada Lou Levin* ∾

I have a second granddaughter. She will be brave, strong, and kind and she will be loved beyond measure. Her world is full of unknowns but her home is one of devotion and safety. She was born in the same hospital that her father was, thirty-seven years before. She will forever be "born in San Diego"—2770 miles away from her sister's birthplace.

There's no good time to end a long story about the struggles we faced in 2020 and 2021 and all that COVID put us through. It's become pretty clear that we can't end the story when the virus is gone. It seems to have fierce staying power.

So, tiny, beautiful Ada Lou, I choose this day—the day you were born to parents whose image you first saw wearing a mask—as the end of this story.

I have another granddaughter. It's time to write another book.

∾

About the Author

These days, Gail Vetter Levin can throw a mean tea party and bring animation to *Moo, Baa, La, La, La* and *Goodnight Moon*. And there's nothing she'd rather do. But it wasn't always fun and games.

A longtime San Diegan, Gail's career paths have taken her from the halls of Poway High as an English teacher to the halls of Congress as a Press Secretary. She wrote speeches for the Congressional Record and scripts for the local Emmy awards. She's ripped and read copy on Channel 13 News in Las Vegas and compiled complicated funding requests as a leader with local and national non-profits.

When Covid-19 struck, Gail hunkered down with her husband, Marty, and set about recording how it all felt — especially the distance between her granddaughter and herself. So far, that has proven to be the writing that matters to her the most.

Acknowledgements

It has taken me a long time to say the words, "I'm writing a book." It will take me even longer to say, "I've written a book" but, in fact, there is a book and it has my name where the author's name goes. This is something I have always wanted to do. Good or bad, interesting or dull—I have written a book and I thank all of you who have encouraged me and those who will take the time to read it.

Special thanks to Marilyn who helped me bust out the writer that I've always wanted to be and to my writing buddies, Carrie and Connie, for their wise and witty counsel. To Sue, who cheered me at the beginning and read line by line to the end—all for the better. To Cousin Nancy, who held the step stool so I could get down off my high horse, at least a little.

Thanks to friends, here and gone, who have given me stories to write and then encouraged me to share— Martha, Mark, Gail, Tom, Ken, Ingrid, Susan, Barbara, Jill, Cindy, Alicia, Kim, Robin, and Alice.

Thanks to my son who has given me fodder for writing through his whole life because he's wonderful and funny; to my remarkable daughter-in-law, who made me a grandmother and brought her beautiful girls to play in the Pacific.

Thank you to Marty, who has always held my hand and my heart and who said yes to this project along with many others that made even less sense.

Finally, to those who had to do the heavy lifting through this unique time and to the thousands of souls we lost in the pandemic. May their memory be a blessing.

Made in the USA
Columbia, SC
13 June 2024

37127505R00124